MAKING
PARTNER

MAKING PARTNER

A GUIDE FOR LAW FIRM ASSOCIATES

ROBERT MICHAEL GREENE

American Bar Association
Section of Law Practice Management

© 1992 American Bar Association.
All rights reserved.
Printed in the United States of America.

Library of Congress Number: 91-76632
ISBN: 0-89707-730-X

91 92 93 94 95 5 4 3 2 1

Discounts are available for books ordered in bulk. Special consideration is given to state bars, CLE programs, and other bar-related nonprofit organizations. Inquire at Publications Planning and Marketing, American Bar Association, 750 North Lake Shore Drive, Chicago, Illinois 60611.

For Amy, Megan,
Timothy, and Daniel

CONTENTS

CONTENTS

CONTENTS

ACKNOWLEDGMENTS

I wish to thank Judy Grubner, Rick Feferman, Beth Heid, Jane Johnston, Mark Ingebretsen, Gary Munneke, Paula Tsurutani, Sharon Winchell, and Paul Zuydhoek for their suggestions for improvements, their patience with me, and their assistance in making my idea a reality.

Without their encouragement, this book would not have happened.

INTRODUCTION

How much do you know about the rules of roulette . . . or baccarat . . . or even blackjack? If you are like me and probably most other law school graduates, the answer is very little. Oh, we have a rudimentary knowledge of these games—probably just enough to be able to lose whatever we are willing to gamble on infrequent visits to casinos. But I will bet you do not know the odds of winning or all the intricate rules of the house. We just like to sit on the stool, looking more experienced, more sophisticated, and wealthier than we are, convincing ourselves and those with us that it is fun.

I have written this book because I am concerned that many law school students entering private practice as associates are approaching their careers in much the same way. We (I will be presumptuous and rejoin your ranks) ask all the wrong questions when being interviewed by firms, then repeat the mistake after being hired by not learning the "rules of the house" for making partner.

This book offers some general guidelines to help you invest your time wisely. I will presume the cards are just being dealt. If you do not think you are on track, after reading this little book, maybe you will consider starting the game over again, at least in some respects.

Admittedly, it has been a few years since I was in the Partnership Sweepstakes. But it is one of those things I will never forget, particularly because every day I see energetic, well-intentioned, enthusiastic associates doing the same things I did.

The relevance of this book to you will depend on all sorts of factors I cannot predict. The health of the local economy, the size of your firm, luck, your personal financial clout, and many other matters too numerous to list will play a part. But all things being equal (which they never are), my suggestions will have some importance to you. You will have to adapt them to your circumstances. For example, if you are with a small firm—say, fewer than 10 lawyers—it is harder to implement my recommendations on information gathering inconspicuously. But the answers you need are probably more obvious anyway.

At times you may think I am preaching. I am. I have a lot to say and want to get it said in a book of manageable length. It would probably be kinder of me to make my points by using examples or analogies. But you and I are interested in the end result—partnership for you— so I tend to be blunt and skip the niceties. I apologize if I offend.

1

BE WELL INFORMED

The local legal community was amazed. The Chicago firm's demise was not so surprising, because its major client was a bank that had been taken over by the regulators. When over half your work comes directly or indirectly from one source, it is difficult to survive the loss of that client. No, the surprising part to all—including the associates at the firm—was the disclosures made in court proceedings regarding the firm itself. Everyone believed 27 partners practiced under the firm's double name. But only in the liquidation did everyone learn that the double name reflected the firm's real structure. There were only two true partners. All the others who bore that title were employees, on salary and without a say in the firm's governance.

Choosing a new partner is admittedly more complex than buying a microwave, but like the buyers of appliances, law firms shopping for a future partner seek value for their dollar. They want the best they can get, and they look for someone who has demonstrated that he or she will be an asset to the firm and its practice.

As an aspiring partner, how do you do that? How do you demonstrate that you will be an asset to your law firm? How do you gauge its needs, hone your talents to match those needs, and then catch the eye of the prime decision-makers? The first step is to learn your job and what is expected of you by gathering as much information as possible.

To succeed at that, you will need two very different kinds of information. First, you must learn about the law firm. This chapter discusses finding out about your firm, its policies and procedures, and the general qualities any law firm looks for in a partner. Second, you must learn about the political realities in your firm—the kind of information you will need to play your cards to best advantage in the quest for partnership—to be covered in later chapters.

FIRM OPERATIONS, POLICIES, AND PROCEDURES

Your law firm should try to give you information about its operations, policies, and procedures through an organized orientation program. This program will allow you to ask questions and learn the firm's official responses. (I say "official" because in most law firms, practice does not always reflect official policy. You will learn the actual practice over time from the people in the law firm, including a cynical partner, your peers, and even your secretary. Do your utmost to adhere to official policy — it is always safer.)

In a small firm the orientation program may consist of a lengthy meeting or two with a partner and/or a nuts-and-bolts session with a well-seasoned secretary. These orientations are probably the best, because they give you plenty of opportunity to ask questions and revisit areas as you become integrated into the firm.

In slightly larger firms, a commonly used method for introducing new lawyers is to assign a mentor to the new associate from the ranks of the senior associates. This is a good way to learn about office politics as well as policy on an ongoing basis.

If your law firm does not provide either an orientation or a mentor, consider asking for a mentor anyway, whether your firm is large or small. It shows enthusiasm on your part and can help you adjust to private practice at your new firm.

Also read and digest any manual provided to associates or other employees. Most well-run large law firms will have a manual for lawyers and support staff. You should know what it says and keep it updated as new policies are published. Despite the comments you will hear describing the manual as out-of-date or aspirational, it will give you a good overview of office policies. And if the firm bothered to publish the manual, it obviously was important to someone involved in the firm's future and yours. So until you are advised otherwise by someone in authority, presume that the manual states the rules.

Another good source of information will be your supervising lawyer or department head. After all, he or she is part of firm management and responsible for you. Never worry about asking a "stupid" question. It is far better to ask than to guess wrong. Your supervisor is just as interested in seeing you get off on the right foot as you are. Remember that your supervisor is evaluated and compensated according to how well the department operates. And you are now part of that well-oiled machine.

QUESTIONS TO ASK

Here is a partial list of some of the questions you should ask when you are new to a law firm:

- How many hours am I expected to devote to the practice? How many of those hours must be billable to clients? Am I expected regularly to work evenings or appear in the office on weekends?

- When are time sheets due, and how is compliance monitored?

- If I have a piece of new business, what approvals do I need before I may accept the engagement? What process is used to avoid conflicts of interest?

- Am I expected to take on any office management responsibilities? If so, how do I account for the time? (Such jobs include serving as the managing clerk who logs in litigation notices, giving tours to recruits visiting the office, and being available in the office during lunch hours.)

- Am I expected to be involved in civic or professional activities? If so, how do I account for the time? Will I be assisted in getting involved, or am I on my own?

- When I travel for clients or the law firm, or serve on civic or bar committees, what expenses are reimbursable?

- How will I be given work assignments? Am I fair game for any partner going by my office, or are there channels to be followed? May other associates assign me work directly?

- What reports are expected from me with respect to pending work assignments, the status of files, etc.?

- What type of client contact am I afforded? May I write to, meet with, and talk to clients directly? If so, how soon?

No doubt there are many other questions you should ask, but this list is a start. The answers will give you a basis for starting to function in the office. As you become more oriented over time, your list of questions relating to operations will grow and become more complex. Just keep asking! As I said earlier, there is no harm in asking, just in guessing wrong.

CRITERIA FOR PARTNERSHIP

Law firms rarely publish the criteria for partnership, although some have. If you ask some of the partners, you will probably get the same answer, more or less, but with varying emphasis. The emphasis will change from partner to partner and from time to time, but large office or small, the criteria are much the same.

Personal Characteristics

Written criteria or a thoughtful response from a partner will probably include most of the following personal characteristics:

- *Hard work*—This is usually expressed in terms of number of hours devoted to the practice, i.e., billable hours, practice development hours, training efforts, and management contribution, but particularly billable hours.

- *Good work*—This means you research, write, speak, and negotiate well. You are technically proficient and have good practice habits.

- *Client-handling skills*—You handle clients well and are able to convince them you are handling their matters well — so well, in fact, that they relish being billed for your efforts.

- *Maturity*—You are in control of your life. You receive, as well as merit, the respect of colleagues, adversaries, staff, and others.

- *Public profile*—You are involved in your community and profession in a way that reflects well on yourself and the law firm.

- *Collegiality*—You are pleasant to be with and contribute to a positive atmosphere in the office. You fit.

- *Entrepreneurial attitude*—You think like an owner rather than an employee. You are willing to invest your energy, your ideas, and your money in the future of the law firm.

- *Client development*—Because you meet the other criteria, existing clients ask you to do more work for them, and new clients seek you to represent them.

- *Need of the law firm*—There is a space for you, and the law firm needs to fill that space. Admittedly, this criterion is a curve ball, because you have little, if any, control over it. Deaths, retirements, and partner defections create need. Likewise, industry trends and client reactions to those trends can create or eliminate need. The financial management of the practice, and its prosperity, will most often determine whether the partners are willing to let you sit by their pie with fork in hand.

Criteria Relating to Firm Need

Besides the personal criteria, there are criteria reflecting the law firm's need for new partners. You should know these criteria, too, because they influence the process or the timetable for making partner. Criteria relating to the firm's need include these items:

- *Mandatory retirement*—Does the law firm have a program that requires partners who reach a specified age to give up their units, management/practice control, or other responsibilities? Or are they all permitted to hang on until their health or mental acuity decline to an unacceptable level? Obviously, the former policy is to your advantage. If partners are dropping off systematically at the far end, there is more likely to be space for you at the front.

- *Firm structure* —Is there a single tier of partners in the firm? Or are there multiple tiers?

7

What is the track? Are junior partners or nonequity partners made after a few years, with full, equity, or senior partnership held off for another period of apprenticeship (or perhaps forever)?

▪ *Growth policy* — Does the law firm intend to grow over time? Is there a plan for achieving such growth? Does the plan include hiring and training new associates, hiring laterals, or merging with other firms, or all three? If lateral hires are introduced, how does this affect the partnership prospects of "home-grown" associates?

▪ *Partner power* —Once you are an equity, full, general, senior, fully ensconced partner, what rights do you have? Is voting weighted? Is it so heavily weighted that a few or even a very few partners control the firm, firm decisions, and partner compensation? What matters come to the partners for decision? Are all important issues delegated to a select few without appeal? Does the partnership agreement structure decision making so that the governing body is unfettered?

▪ *Governance*—Is the governing body effective? Can any partner run for the governing body, or are there criteria based on years of partnership, level of compensation, or heredity?

These questions the firm asks about its needs really go to the issue of what partnership is in your law firm or prospective law firm. Be aware that with the pressures the law business is under these days, your firm may be reevaluating its answers. For example, your firm may be considering adding a new tier (with tears!) to the partnership. Or it may decide to designate some associates as senior lawyers who are very welcome but may not become partners, or staff lawyers who are hired on the understanding that they will never be in the race for partnership but will perform basic, routine legal services. Or the partnership track may be lengthened by years for all prospects. However, if partners have very little say in firm matters, firm management may feel there is no harm in adding a few more.

Each of these strategies is designed to limit the number of partners, defer their canonization, or make the position of little consequence. The principle is like the approach to paying taxes: Tomorrow is better than today, because I can use the money today. The partners take the same view of the gold they divide or the power they share: Tomorrow is better for creating new partners than today, because it means fewer people with whom to share today.

These questions may be even tougher in very small firms where there may be room for you only when a partner dies, retires, or otherwise leaves. If that is the case, you should know it before you invest time, energy, and ability for the sake of the firm.

As to the issue of governance, some law firms have departed or are considering departing from the more or less democratic structures that were relatively popular in the past, particularly with small firms. In a mature market-driven industry, which law is today, more "businesslike" decision-making methods are being adopted

—i.e., the hierarchy is higher and steeper. Being a partner just ain't what it used to be!

Most firms have discussed, are discussing, or will discuss some aspects of these strategies. You need to know whether you are likely to be affected, and why and how. These answers will not be easy to get.

WHY NOT ASK?

To be informed about how these issues will affect you, as a law school student you should consider asking the questions outlined in Appendix A when being interviewed. However, it is unlikely that many students have thought to ask or have had the audacity to ask these questions about partnership structure and law firm management. Nevertheless, the few times I have been asked about these issues while on the interviewing circuit, I have been impressed and have had no problem answering the queries as best I could.

Perhaps some day law firms will include such information in their hiring brochures. Why? Well, it would be nice to know what stakes you are playing for and who makes the rules of the game. But it is highly unlikely that firms will do so readily. That would be paramount to giving away the secret code words. Therefore, you will have to ask.

"Oh, man, I can't ask about *that!*"

Sure you can, if you know how. It is acceptable (although perhaps a tad audacious) for you to ask these questions during your interview. If you didn't ask, however, and are already working, you must pursue this information patiently and diplomatically. And here are a few suggestions you should consider:

Generally your peers are the worst source for accurate information about much of anything relating to firm matters other than the location of the rest rooms. Every firm has an associate or staff rumor mill, which embellishes and enhances mistaken information as it makes the rounds of the office. Using it as a source of intelligence is much like playing "telephone" with a group of small children. After a story is whispered from ear to ear around a table, the final version rarely resembles the original one.

But I know you will ask anyway, so go ahead. Ask your peers. Just do not believe the answers. They will contain an element of truth, but rarely an accurate depiction of the entire situation.

Make up your own list of questions that have been inspired by what you have read so far, your own curiosity, or rumors you have heard. Do it carefully and thoughtfully, much as you would prepare interrogatories. Arrange the questions logically from the general to the specific.

Do not make an appointment with the managing partner to answer under oath all your questions not addressed by the firm's handbook or policy memos. (Managing partners do not lie. They are just so shell-shocked they become disoriented.) Rather, wait until you can ask the question naturally in the course of a conversation. On the way to court, walking along Main Street, with one of the partners over a beer, at lunch, on the airplane — if one of your questions fits into the conversation, ask it casually and offhandedly. If the partner is responsive and appears willing to enter into a dialogue, throw in a related question or press gingerly for more detail. Do not overdo it. Do not be aggressive.

Just go far enough to maximize the opportunity without being pushy.

The next time such an opportunity arises, ask a different question. If you want to compare responses of different partners to the same question, let some time pass so you do not draw attention to yourself as pressing on a particular topic.

Take your time; you will probably need a few years to get answers to all your questions. The answers you receive will beget new questions. Remember that you do not have to know everything at once. No matter how good you are, it is unlikely that you will be seriously considered for partnership the first year or so out of law school. I am sorry to disappoint you.

You do not have to be alone with a partner to ask a question. If others hear, so what? At the same time, do not insist that it be a group conversation; remember, you are just slipping the questions into a personal conversation.

During this process, it is important to comport yourself as an associate interested in the firm and its future, not as a pushy lawyer trying to become a candidate as soon as possible. Your questions should be generic, not personal. They should not be accusatory or adversarial, but rather purely informational. If your firm has no-holds-barred question-and-answer sessions for associates, ask a question or two, but do not go overboard. Do not monopolize the meeting. You may hurt yourself in the eyes of your peers and the participating partners. Few people really like a pushy lawyer . . . particularly another lawyer.

2

RELAX

The young lawyer had never encountered an ego quite so grand before. Actually it was a cover used by a terribly insecure senior partner. But the ego had to be fed, had to be exercised by regular abuse of younger lawyers. The senior lawyer set unreasonable deadlines and questioned conclusions in a manner that pushed his insecurity onto the junior practitioner.

The result was predictable. The junior lawyer worked more intensely, triple-checking good work unnecessarily and conducting research endlessly because there was always another possibility to consider. Work never ended; hobbies faded; family and friends were ignored.

The cycle stopped for the young lawyer only when he was hospitalized with an ulcer. The senior partner's response was that an ulcer is the badge of a successful practice.

Once you have begun gathering information about the firm, its structure, its partnership, its criteria, and so on, what do you do with all the data? Nothing. Just file it away.

Do not prepare a strategic plan for becoming a partner. Do not create a time line or fix a goal.

No matter how friendly you may become with any partner, do not seek advice on how to advance your cause.

If the firm does not have written criteria for partnership, do not organize an effort to get them developed.

Why not? Because you will be trying too hard, and it will show. You will be viewed as presumptuous. Your efforts may backfire. To the degree you have any control over your destiny, you will lose it.

In any office, large or small, there are many factors over which you have no say. For example, the firm's financial fortunes, retirements or deaths of partners, the arrival of laterals or departure of partners, and the shifting needs of the marketplace are all beyond your control.

Certainly, be as informed as you can about foreseeable events in the law firm. This may give you an opportunity to help—an important message to send to management.

Relax, store up information on the firm, and start to focus on the matters you can control. But what are these? Please read on. That is what the rest of this book is about.

A LIFE OTHER THAN WORK

Part of relaxing is to have a multidimensional life. The quest for partnership is important to you, but the activities discussed in the remaining chapters of this book should not be the most important thing in your life—happiness should be, and partnership should be just one component of your happiness.

Be careful to avoid letting the quest for partnership consume your life and its focus. This means you should actively maintain interests outside the office. Get involved in dance, antiquing, handball, yoga, or mountain climbing, something that will refresh and relax you and develop a new dimension in you. Otherwise, you run the risk of becoming obsessed, a workaholic, and generally disliked.

You are at an age when many young professionals are seeking a life partner or forming a relationship with one. The Partnership Sweepstakes should not destroy that for you. You must take time for your spouse and for your family. That necessary diversion does wonders for relaxing.

STRESS MANAGEMENT

At times practice is too demanding, and you will give up a day with your family or a class you were promising yourself. The pressure may even endure, and you will have to turn to the popular remedies prescribed under the rubric of stress management. There are plenty of books and frequent seminars on the subject. Try them. The techniques they offer will help you relax before the race.

To summarize, it is important that you consistently maintain a whole-life focus, and address this issue at each stage of your development. I will say more on this as the book progresses.

3

BE A STUDENT

It was a small find with big consequences. Doing her regular reading of advance sheets, the litigator discovered a sizable verdict against the manufacturer whose press her own client had just purchased.

The litigator had learned about the press during a client visit she had scheduled as a hunting expedition for new work. She had taken a look at the press to satisfy the client's mix of pride and frustration. Then, over lunch in the company cafeteria, the client had recited a litany of complaints about start-up problems with the press.

After reading the advance sheet report, the litigator made a phone call to the successful lawyer in the case for guidance. That call produced a new case for the young litigator and a lucrative solution to her client's press problems.

If you chose to practice law because you like to think and study, you chose well. Knowledge is your stock in trade. Certainly you must understand the law you practice, but you must also commit yourself to learning about the world in general. Staying abreast of developments within the profession will help your work and personal growth, and broad knowledge will make you more attractive to the partners in your firm. In short, always be a student — of the law, of your clients, of the profession, of your community, and of yourself.

THE LAW

An adage observes that a recent law school graduate will never know more law and never know less about what to do with it. If you are going to succeed as a lawyer, you must never stop reading and studying the law. This will involve reading recent court decisions, law review articles, ethics opinions, the newsletters and updates published on various areas of specialty, and statutory changes — all regularly. It will mean attending seminars regularly. It will mean watching videotapes at home and listening as you drive to cassettes on everything from substantive areas of law and practice management to practice techniques and ethics.

This constant updating of self must be general; you must have a general notion of what is going on in the law—what cases the Supreme Court is deciding, what the Congress and your state legislatures are doing. But the longer you are in practice, whether your firm is large or small, you will, and should, start to specialize. This may happen by design if you are assigned to a particular department or receive particular types of cases. Or it may be happenstance because of a particular success and the work that flows from it. Offices large and small have various degrees of specialization or restrict their practice areas. As you specialize, the reading, the study, the seminars will follow.

Aside from all the reading, watching, and listening you do by yourself, you will get your best education as you work with seasoned lawyers. All you need is one.

Vent your curiosity by watching how work is done, by looking at work product. Ask to go along to the closing or the pretrial examination. Ask questions during unused breaks in the proceedings or later on the way back to the office.

Ask if you can try what the more experienced lawyer is doing. Take a step and ask to take another. Ask, try, ask, try! Push until you are cautioned to slow down. But never stop pushing, experimenting, trying, learning from others doing, learning from doing yourself. Whoever dubbed the law a "practice" said it accurately. It will never change for the creative lawyer. Your career will be a flow of such trying, experimenting, and learning by doing.

This approach will set you apart from the many who find it more comfortable to follow. Admittedly what I suggest is riskier. You will fall on your face a time or two, but you will learn from that as well. And the rewards are greater. The followers will be nice and safe . . . somewhere behind you.

At no time in your career should this process of self-education stop. You will need it to make partner, to be a successful lawyer, to be a successful partner.

THE CLIENTS

Like the litigator in the opening vignette, you must also be a student of your clients and of their industries. Being knowledgeable about the business trends affecting clients will enhance your ability to represent them and will endear you to them. By understanding the pressures clients are under and the factors affecting their industries, you will be able to foresee problems, understand the context within which problems arise, and know what others comparably situated are doing. You will know the jargon of your client and be better able to communicate.

How can you do this? Again, reading is a key ingredient. *The Wall Street Journal* is a regular source on business matters on the large scale. The local press and local business press also help. On-line computer databases enable you to track clients' doings and those of their competitors. So do trade journals and newsletters.

Also get out of your office and look around. A tour of a client's facility, seeing it operate, is a great orientation. Attending trade shows or conventions can be the ultimate step.

The time and effort needed to educate yourself in a client's industry must be justified by the amount of work received from that client. You will not have time to keep fully abreast of all industries at all times. With the demands on your time, you must be selective. (Knowing your client and its business will also be important for marketing, discussed in Chapter 10.)

THE COMMUNITY

You should know and have some understanding of the economic, political, and social forces affecting your community. What companies are key players? Who leads them? Are there racial tensions? Which political party controls, and who controls that party? Does the newspaper have a bias; if so, what is it? What is the breakdown according to religious affiliation?

Remember that any client problem will have to fit within the context of the community. These factors will have influence whether you are picking a jury or negotiating a contract.

If you were raised in the community in which you practice, you may be too ready to assume you know this information. You certainly have an advantage, but you must keep current. If you are a recent transplant, you will have to scramble to pick it up.

Your first and best source is the local press. Older natives in the firm will be of valuable assistance. They usually love to drone on about their hometown and all the background information you need. Just ask. We will return to this topic in Chapter 10.

THE PROFESSION

Read about trends in the profession. This will help you and the firm maximize opportunities and avoid problems. Several general publications are worth your time. *The National Law Journal* (New York: New York Law Publishing Co.) and *American Lawyer* (New York: American Lawyer Media, L.P.) are popular. There are also several nontabloid publications worth considering. *Of Counsel* (Englewood Cliffs, New Jersey: Prentice-Hall Law & Business) and *Law Office Management & Administration Report* (New York: Institute of Management & Administration, Inc.) are quite good. These publications are not inexpensive but are found in most large law offices. If your firm subscribes, get on the circulation list. If not, check out your local law library.

As with everything else, do not take what the tabloids report as gospel. There will always be exaggerations, tactical denials, etc. But these publications are good at giving you a feel for how various markets are doing—what's hot and what's not, what pressures other firms are feeling, and what is being done about them.

In your early years of "associatedom," it is highly unlikely that you will be able to react to this information. But you will be able to observe intelligently as your firm reacts. You also will be able to ask questions more pointedly as you build up your storehouse of information on the firm and its practice.

Do not fall into the trap of assuming your firm is a mirror image of the marketplace, buffeted exactly as described in the legal press. There will always be variations and exceptions. What is important is to know whether your firm is riding a wave along with many others or swimming against the current—successfully, I hope.

Do not worry or become overconfident if your practice area is described as weak or one of the strongest. If your firm is doing well in real estate when real estate is soft and management wants you to practice real estate law, go for it. Trying to ride major trends in the marketplace within the context of your firm is useless and foolish. Even if you could do it, which is unlikely, you will bounce around like the ball on a roulette wheel for no particular benefit. Rather, practice where you are needed and where you enjoy the work. That is the crucial combination for your practice and for the firm.

On the other hand, if you see that an area of interest to you and to clients is heating up, do not hesitate to suggest boning up in expectation of new business opportunities. You can hit pay dirt if the work materializes; if it does not, you have broadened your intellect and impressed the partners with your business instincts and your interest in the future of the firm. Making such recommendations is not a must by any means, but it is the way forward-thinking lawyers develop. It will not happen as you walk in the door. It may be years or may never happen at all—but keep a weather eye open for the opportunity.

Be mindful that your new area of expertise does not have to be a whole new area of practice for the firm. This can occur within a specialty or subspecialty in which you have been asked to practice. For example, if you are asked to be a real estate practitioner, the possibility of working into a condominium practice may be an opportunity in your market. Or your specialization may be even more restrictive, such as representing homeowner associations created by condominium developers.

If you take this route, do not fret if the partners politely turn down your offer. They know or should know the market better than you do. They may have already examined the possibilities. Your suggestion may not fit within the firm's strategic plan. Even so, you certainly do not lose points for suggesting. Quite the contrary. You should not feel discouraged about trying again if you come up with another idea.

Nevertheless, do not become a fountain of ideas for new practice areas. If you come up with an idea, fine. But you should not become the source of monthly memoranda to the managing partner filled with your analysis of the marketplace and the firm's future.

(I will say more on how to make suggestions in Chapter 6.)

YOURSELF

As you start practice and then develop as a lawyer, you must monitor yourself. No lawyer is uniformly creative and an expert in all aspects of being a lawyer. There is always some aspect that can be improved upon, whether it is research skills, writing or speaking ability, negotiation ability, or bedside manner. You have to identify what it is.

Feedback on Assignments

In the early stages of your career, there will be plenty of assignments, usually written, coming from more experienced lawyers. Ask for feedback as you complete projects. Did you deliver what they wanted? More? Less? How could your work be improved? Any suggestions for the next time?

You will discover that some lawyers are better than others at providing meaningful feedback. You may get "fine" and a new assignment from one partner, while another will go over your work product line by line with a red pen. No matter. Keep asking, and compare the input you receive from different partners. Sometimes reconciling advice will be difficult, as lawyers have differing styles. But keep ingesting their comments, and learn from what they tell you.

Associate Evaluations

Law firms have devised a unique form of torture known as the "associate evaluation." Usually performed at least annually, it is normally based on the homogenized input received from the partners with whom you have labored. Take this experience and use it to your advantage.

Listen carefully, taking in everything.

Ask questions in order to get as clear a picture as possible.

Do not complain or try to explain away any negative feedback. Some of it will hurt, but you must look past the pain to make the adjustments the firm wants. Simply put, if the firm wants a correction, you will have to make it if you are going to be a partner in the firm.

When the interview is over and while it is still fresh in your memory, take notes for later study. If on later review of your notes more questions arise, go ask them.

As you work on subsequent assignments, ask whether you have improved on the points raised in your evaluation.

The longer you are with the firm, the higher the standard that will be applied in your evaluations. They will get tougher because you are supposed to be progressing. Remember, however, that this torture is intended to help you move along the path to partnership. The firm wants you to succeed. It has invested much time, effort, and money in you. That is why people are telling you what is expected of you, what you need to do to succeed. Listen.

4

WORK HARD

No one could figure out what was wrong. The associate came in right after dropping off her children at day care about 7:00 A.M., and she rarely left before 7:00 P.M. to pick them up. (The office joke was that she really didn't like them.) But she was averaging only about 100 chargeable hours each month, even though plenty of work was available and her work was timely.

Only after one of the older hands observed her on one of his projects did things change. He bought her a watch (with a built-in stopwatch feature to force a laugh) so she could stop guessing how much time she had spent on each project. And he reiterated that she was to report actual time spent without adjustment for her own view of its worth. Valuation was part of the bill-rendering process, not her time-recording process. The next month, the associate's chargeable hours approached 160 without any change in her schedule.

As in this vignette, the big bugaboo for private practitioners today is the chargeable hour — or, more accurately, the number of chargeable hours. Most lawyers will confess that they are paid on a "piecework" basis; the more units they manufacture, the more they are paid. The units in this case are hours of legal work.

27

Unfortunately, this view is accurate. Quantity rather than quality is the unit of measurement currently in vogue. We are all captives of it, though I have yet to meet a lawyer who truly likes this monster we have created for ourselves.

While other approaches to billing, such as value billing, are being examined currently, you will not be in a position as an associate to change the system. The partners are unlikely to have this opportunity. So do not try. Just learn how the system works at your firm, then use it to the advantage of yourself and the firm.

The most painful part of billing based on chargeable hours is the need for daily time sheets. Although firms differ in how they collect the data, the basic need to report how you spend your workday is common to all. And that need is like the body's requirement for regular nourishment; it never takes a break. But more on that later.

If you want to become a partner as soon as you can, you will have to work hard and make sure that the partners know that you are working hard. You can do that by following the guidelines in this chapter.

KNOW WHAT IS EXPECTED

As I outlined in Chapter 1, find out what is expected of you. The orientation process, the firm manual, your mentor, or a time-budgeting procedure should have given you some hint of the firm's expectations regarding how many hours you are to devote to client matters, practice development activities, continuing legal education, management, vacation, etc. Just make sure your information is current.

BUDGET YOUR TIME

Once you know what is expected of you, budget your time. Many well-managed firms use time budgeting as a part of the financial budgeting process and as a means of agreeing with lawyers about how much effort is to be devoted to the practice and where the effort is to be placed.

Each firm will have its own requirements for what to include in a time budget. Typically, the budget will itemize responsibility for billable time, practice development, and management duties.

Sample Budget

Even if your firm does not require a specific budget, I suggest you use this budgeting process to help organize your practice and put your daily effort into perspective. For example, assume you must meet the following expectations:

- 2,000 billable hours annually

- participation in at least one bar association panel for 50 hours per year and one local civic group for another 75 hours per year

- conducting tours and having lunch with recruits 10 to 15 times at two hours each

- research for an article being written by one of the partners, as well as participation in an in-office training program for clients on the same subject for a total of 100 hours

- handling a pro bono case assigned by the Volunteer Lawyer's Project

- attendance at one or more two-day CLE seminars

If all this is true, you will have a time budget that looks roughly like this:

TIME BUDGET

Billable hours		2,000
Practice development:		
Research for article	100	
Civic group	75	
Bar panel	50	225
CLE		16
Pro bono case		60
Management		30
Total		2,331

Assume further that you will lose five workdays to illness or personal leave and will take two weeks' vacation and nine holidays. This leaves you with 237 workdays, not counting weekends. Applying my skills at long division, it looks as though a typical workday will include 8.4 billable hours and 1.4 hours of practice development. You will have to work in your CLE courses and management responsibilities as scheduled, but expressed as an average day, they represent only fractions of an hour.

Of course, this budget does not account for time studying advance sheets or law newsletters, opening junk mail, getting coffee, listening to a senior partner recount war stories (a la the Bungalow murders of

Horace Rumpole), planning the associate holiday party, spreading rumors about a partner's peccadillo, asking the questions I suggested in Chapter 1, retrieving a lost file, or the hundreds of other little things that fill your days. In my experience, these ancillary activities come to 50 percent of the time billed. Thus, to put in 8.4 billable hours, you can expect to spend an additional 4.2 hours in the office. This means you can count on 12- to 13-hour days and 65-hour weeks.

Organization of Time

Be mindful that your day will not be as neatly organized as the sample budget implies. Wish that it were. As you will have whole days given over to a CLE course, likewise you will have a day or days devoted to a practice development effort — for example, attending a client convention or researching the article being written by a senior partner. Other days (and nights and weekends) will be consumed with the generation of billable hours.

Work and assignments do not flow evenly. You do not always work steadily. Some days, billable time is the interruption in a schedule filled with the ancillaries. In fact, that occurs more frequently the more senior you become. At least that is the way it seems.

COMPARE ACTUAL WITH BUDGETED HOURS

Monitor yourself from week to week and month to month against your time budget. Always know whether you are on track to meet the firm's expectations for the year.

Most firms will give you periodic reports. Know them. Study them. If the firm does not generate such information or distribute it to you, then ask your secretary (nicely!) to keep it for you.

If you are on track or ahead of schedule, fine. If you are falling behind, you will have to seek out more assignments.

Ask your supervising lawyer for more work. Let him or her know you will work harder but do not have the work to do. It is a very positive message and will probably cause the firm to reconsider work allocations if someone else is overloaded. Do not worry that by asking you may put yourself out of a job. If work is that unavailable, your asking will only help you by showing your willingness to work when cuts are being made. The only wrong thing to do is to chug along at less than full speed without asking for more work.

KEEP ACCURATE TIME RECORDS

Evaluate your timekeeping practices. You should record the necessary information for your time sheets as the day progresses. Much billable time is lost because the timekeeper is trying to remember what was accomplished a day or two after the fact. You simply cannot remember every substantive telephone call, letter, or quick research project. And if you do remember them, you will not necessarily recall the amount of time spent. As with the lawyer in the opening vignette, the natural human instinct is to downgrade the amount of time and the importance of your effort as time passes. So record each task right away, as you do it.

Note well that I do not suggest you do anything to inflate your time. That is immoral, unethical, and ultimately may cost the firm its client relationship.

When I say "inflate time," I am referring to the many neat tricks that allow the timekeeper to avoid feeling guilty, but that are intellectually dishonest. For example, someone might say, "I arrived at 8:00 A.M., took an hour for lunch, and left at 5:30 P.M. That's 8.5 hours in the office. I may have spent one-half hour on the mail and getting coffee, so I must divide the 8.0 hours remaining among my client efforts for the day." Such filling in the gaps is never accurate. There are many more interruptions you must allow for. No one who is being honest works 8.0 billable hours in an 8.5-hour workday spent in the office. It will probably be closer to 6.0 or 7.0 billable hours if you are really pressing. When in court or traveling for a client, actually working those 8.0 hours is a bit easier.

Do not kid yourself or cheat the client! But also remember that by recording each client matter as it arises, you will not let anything slip by. You and your firm are entitled to that.

Do not evaluate or weight your time as you record it. If a research job took 11.6 hours one day, write it down. If the end product is not worth that much, the billing lawyer will make the necessary adjustment. That is not for you to do. All legitimate effort should be recorded at full time expended. You should not include items that are a wasted effort, such as searching for your lost file or trying but failing to place a telephone call.

I have always kept a pad on my desk next to the telephone for recording time sheet entries. That way I can record each call as it comes in or goes out. I build my time sheet as the day progresses, checking at several intervals during the day to make sure it is complete.

BE FLEXIBLE

Part of working hard and working the requisite number of billable hours will mean having a flexible schedule. You will sometimes have to work early mornings, late evenings, and weekends. Do not assume that the "all-nighter" went out when you graduated from law school.

But go to such lengths only when it is necessary. Do not do it for show. If there is a deadline, if the client has a time-sensitive need, if a load of work has backed up, then get the job done. No one will score you highly if you simply play to the audience without cause. You are entitled to be appreciated for extraordinary effort. But if you are going to extraordinary lengths without justification, people will quickly determine this. At best they will think you strange. At worst they will question your motives or your stability.

When extra effort is required, work with a smile. Do not complain. Do not be a martyr. If others are working at your side, they probably do not want to be there either. No one likes a complainer. Rather, people avoid complainers even in times of extreme need.

If you are not directly involved in a major project that is requiring herculean efforts by the office, volunteer to help. You certainly will be appreciated for trying. And if the day comes when you are living at the office on a project, you will have more ready volunteers. This is especially true in small firms or practice groups.

Your smile, your attitude, and your willingness to volunteer will also be important to team building, as discussed in Chapter 6. They are mentioned here because they will help you get the work and the hours you need. People like to work with people they like. They will pick you first when help is needed. You want them to pick you first when picking partners, too.

All this off-hours activity will be particularly difficult for the primary caregiver of young children or older relatives. You must develop a backup system in the event you cannot get home or pick up at day care as scheduled. Clients with problems do not care about such issues or whether you do not feel well or have too much work to do. The lawyers in your office will be sympathetic and try to be helpful (I hope!), but they will have their own scheduling problems. The best advice is to work it out as quickly and quietly as you can. Different people have different priorities and different problems. It is important that you do not visit your problems on the office. (More on that in Chapter 7.) But without backup arrangements, you will never get the hours you need to succeed.

5

ORGANIZE

The result for the client-defendant was an impressive success. Thanks to his creative research, the associate had produced a recently decided case that clouded the plaintiff's argument regarding liability. A skillful private investigator produced photographs that certainly would cause a jury to wonder about the extent of the injuries. The settlement agreement was tantamount to a withdrawal from the field of battle with a token payment to save face—not bad considering the defendant had originally stood to lose millions.

But the defendant was not happy, and the result was not sweet. He had not understood the legal niceties of what was transpiring, because no one had ever explained the case to him, and the payment seemed to signal defeat. Furthermore, the client was angry when his name was misspelled in the documents and a crucial decimal had to be handwritten in place. His only comment on the associate's performance was to mutter, "Pretty shabby lawyering!"

If you are going to get your work done well and with style, meet your budget for billable hours, and have time for community activities and a personal life outside the office, you must be organized. I mean *really* organized—yourself, your schedule, your work, and your workplace. Furthermore, your organization must be apparent to everyone—clients, partners, associates, support staff, and the world at large.

Why? "My desk may look messy, but I know where everything is." "I know I am late, but I . . ." It all sounds good, but apparent disorganization means a loss of opportunity to impress favorably. A clean desk, an organized schedule, neat work product, and other signs of organization impress clients and partners that you know what you are doing and you are doing it well; thus, you are a star. The fact is, most slobs fail.

YOUR HEALTH AND APPEARANCE

What most people notice first about you is your physical appearance. Your attire should always be neat, clean, and conservative. No one wants to talk to a lawyer about a problem if the lawyer looks as if he or she is going to the track or to a cocktail party. Know what the standard is in your firm, and dress accordingly. If anything, be a tad more conservative.

Many lawyers over 40 grew up in an atmosphere in which women wore skirts to school, while men wore coats and ties. Today in many schools there is little or no dress code. If you have never learned to dress for business, get a consultant, seek guidance from an older lawyer in the office, or read John Molloy, author of *Dress for Success* (New York: Warner Books), who has written extensively on the subject for women and men and whose syndicated column appears regularly in many newspapers. No one who is deciding your future will accept that you never had to "dress for success" before. It will simply be expected.

Once you have the proper clothes, wear them properly. They must be clean and well pressed; today's casual rumpled look is unacceptable. Men's ties must be tied and up to the collar. Suit jackets should be worn whenever clients or other office visitors are about.

Likewise, your personal hygiene must be unquestioned. This one may be the most difficult: stay in good physical shape. Regular strenuous exercise is good for your coping mechanism, your body, and your weight. Excess weight will be a detriment to you, as some partners will view it as a health risk.

If you smoke, quit. Smokers will not care. Non-smokers will hold your smoking against you. It will be viewed as a health hazard, a social detriment, and a smelly nuisance. Besides, quitting may just mean you will be a partner longer.

PRACTICE HABITS

Your personal business habits also must be organized. Here are some guidelines to keep you on track:

- Be on time for meetings and other appointments.

- Stay until the end of meetings.

- Take copious notes during meetings for your own file, if not for the use of others. You cannot remember everything and should not try. One sure way to look disorganized and to lose everyone's confidence is to forget relevant facts.

▪ Do not try to do two things at once. When a client is with you, he or she deserves and is paying for your undivided attention. You should not take calls from another client, your spouse, or the baby-sitter in that client's presence. If there is an emergency, excuse yourself long enough to solve or delegate the problem. Do not sign correspondence, open the mail, or clip your fingernails in front of a client. You will give the impression you are uninterested, a slob, or both.

YOUR SCHEDULE

You will never be able to work 2,300 hours per year and also follow my advice about being on time, staying to the end, and not doing two things at once unless your schedule is in good form. Like your time sheets, your schedule will require regular attention. It will also need planning.

First, get the tools. You should have a calendar for your desk and a duplicate for your purse or pocket. (Be sure to reconcile them daily, and decide with your secretary whether he or she may make appointments for you.) Your calendar will help you remember all your appointments—something you cannot do unaided. It will also be a good tool, in addition to your time sheets, for remembering your activities.

Plan your schedule for the long term as well as day-to-day.

Your week or your day must be organized around getting done that which is critical. Schedule the most important obligations first. Here are some tips for keeping your priorities straight:

- Matters should be taken in order, so matters with the earliest deadline should be addressed first.

- Set aside big blocks of uninterrupted time for time-consuming projects.

- Plan that activities will take more time than you think. This is always true, particularly when you are starting your practice.

- Quiet time for thinking or stress management is important. Plan some into your day. Get some fresh air (if you live in a town that has any). Eat lunch with friends periodically.

- Plan some time to spend with your secretary each day. Properly directed with your priorities established, your secretary will be a bigger help to you.

- Less important matters from a scheduling viewpoint should be put at the end of the day. You can use in-office work on civic activities, reading advance sheets, reading nonclient-related mail, etc., to fill in gaps in your day, or defer these activities if you must. You can't do that with client matters. And in case I have to say it, your social life comes last.

Numerous seminars and books on time management are available. If organizing your schedule proves to be a particular problem, consider one of them. But do not wait until your professional life is out of control. Be vigilant and get help—early if necessary.

While you are getting everything organized, be sure to include time for your vacation. No matter how anxious you are to make a good impression by jump-starting your career, you need a vacation each year. This time for you and your family is necessary for your mental, physical, and family well-being. It will also permit you to approach work with renewed energy and a fresh outlook. No doubt you will see (and hear of) lawyers in your office who never take a vacation because they are workaholics, compulsive, indispensable, etc. That is fine for them, but not for you. Taking that approach will not help your career; it may hurt it as you drain your resources too low without a break.

Although taking a vacation is important, be flexible. You may not be able to take it when you want to. Occasionally a major trial or closing gets in the way. One sure way to make points in the Partnership Sweepstakes is to be willing to change personal plans for the good of the client and the firm. Remember to do it with a smile.

YOUR WORKPLACE

It is impossible to convince any client that you are giving his or her matter careful attention if files and piles of papers are all over your desk or chairs and on the floor along the walls of your office. It makes no difference if you know where everything is—you will never convince the client of that.

Your office should be neat. It should be appealing to visitors. It should be organized to reflect your organized mind, and you should have only one open file on your desk at a time. Why? Clutter will distract you. It will blur your mind's focus as you try to concentrate on a problem, because you will see other important matters awaiting your attention. If you are under pressure, it is a sure way to bring on a panic attack. You can and should work on only one matter at a time, so have only one in your workplace.

Working this way also limits the potential for lost documents. Papers will not end up in the wrong file because a paper clip picked up an additional page.

The client will see you are working on only one matter—his or hers. That will build the client's confidence in your dedication to his or her problem. That is a strong and important message as you build your working relationship with clients. Here are some simple practices that will help you remember as the details mount and your memory fades:

- Have separate file folders for each matter on which you are laboring. Label the files, and as you develop a caseload, develop an index for all the files. Your secretary should work with you on your system and understand it.

- Organize your file cabinets by client, alphabetizing or using the firm's numbering system. Label the drawers.

- Maintain an index of all cases assigned to you. The index should include the status of each case and matters yet to be addressed, dates due, etc. It does not have to be fancy; scribbled notes (if you can read your own writing) are sufficient. Such a tool will permit you to prioritize assignments—addressing the most immediate problem or deadline first, setting aside blocks of time for major undertakings, calling for help if you see that the whole list of assignments is beyond your capacity. This will also be helpful when reporting to your supervising lawyer or asking your mentor for advice regarding practice management.

- Besides your calendar and your index of cases, prepare daily to-do lists of all your assignments, so nothing slips by. Study each day's list as you prioritize the work to be done and fit the work into your calendar. Store the list in your computer or on paper.

- Carry a piece of notepaper or a stick-on note in your pocket calendar. When you are away from your desk, use the notepaper to jot down requests you receive and things you should remember to do. Add these notes to your to-do list periodically.

By following these guidelines, you will impress clients and partners with your attention to detail. That builds confidence. That makes partners.

As you finish a matter, clean the file of unnecessary paper and close it. If it is the way your firm operates, return your work papers and other documents to the central file and forward necessary papers to the client. If there is research or a form you wish to keep for future reference, file it separately from your working files, and maintain an index for such materials so they can be readily found. Your computer is ideal for this purpose.

If you get busy, have to travel, or are away from the office, mail and files will no doubt pile up in your office. It happens to the best-organized people. When that happens, clean everything out some evening or weekend. Simply reexamine every piece of paper on your desk or chair or floor. You will find that some can be filed and others discarded. You can use this opportunity to reprioritize your pending assignments. I usually have to do such a housecleaning about every two to three weeks. It is cathartic.

Maintain a directory of names, addresses, and telephone and fax numbers for clients, government agencies, opposing counsel, and other resources. Your secretary can be a big help in this regard, and it will permit you to avoid pulling and searching the central file or correspondence folder every time you need to work on a matter. Again, a computer can help.

Your office should reflect you and your personality. Decorate it. Use pictures of loved ones, memorabilia, diplomas, a favorite plant. This will help your attitude, as you spend most of your waking hours laboring there. It shows stability and that you feel at home with the firm. You have settled in, perhaps for your career. That is an important message to send to the partners. They want people who feel at home, who have their act together, who organize their offices to live and work at the firm.

YOUR WORK PRODUCT

Just like you, your schedule, and your office, your work product must be neat, complete, accurate, and on time. You and your firm are being paid a lot of money to make it just so. It is expected.

You will not win every matter you handle, but you cannot permit your client to think you did less than your best. Like the client in the opening vignette, clients do not understand the documents and the jargon lawyers use. But they sure can tell if a document is messy, poorly assembled, or late. That is the standard laypersons will apply to your efforts. In a sense, it becomes the most important standard, because at times it is the only one clients understand.

You will not be able to turn out your work product alone. A team will be working with you—the librarian, your secretary, the office messenger, the kid running the photocopier. It is important that you convey to these people in a nice way that you expect only their best effort. They must help you turn out documents without errors, free of any misspellings, wrong citations, poor copies, etc. If people know you expect only the best, they will expect that of themselves. Quality breeds. (More on quality and teamwork in Chapters 6 and 8.)

Notwithstanding everyone's effort, you are still responsible for the final product. Therefore, it is important that you give it the final review, page by page, line by line, word by word. You are the one responsible. If something is wrong or messy, you will be the one who is blamed. "I am sorry" may not be enough. And to blame your secretary or the office messenger, although perhaps deserved, is poor form. You are the one being paid to turn out the work product. You are the team leader. You are responsible.

Of course, mistakes will get by. If they do, report them and fix them. If you catch an error first, fix it first.

If the mistake is caught by another, fix it immediately. Substitute the page, recopy the exhibit, whatever—but do it quickly and willingly. Also apologize, quickly and sincerely. You goofed. Do not cover it up. Admit it and move on with the problem to be solved or deal to be closed. You cannot permit a mistake to put your client, your team, and yourself off balance and out of focus. You have to get back to the main substantive issue. Hopefully, a quick and full apology will do that.

YOUR PERSONAL LIFE

The same organization you bring to your practice you should also bring to your practice development efforts and to your personal life. Schedule all the activities discussed in this book. For example, Chapter 10 describes your client mailing list; make time to prepare one during an evening at home, and schedule an update periodically. So also your personal obligations. Tax returns come around every year, as does holiday shopping. Efficiency in all aspects of your life will make everything easier and give you more free time for unscheduled activity. (In case I need to mention it, you can kiss your partnership prospects good-bye if you do not file your tax returns. The excuse that you were busy on client matters will not work. I will guarantee that.)

Balancing all of the recommendations in this chapter will require a superhero or produce a superhero. It will not be easy, but it will be worthwhile. Many of the suggestions I have made are common sense approaches to managing stress by minimizing it. As I mentioned in Chapter 2, you may wish to pursue other aspects of stress management through courses and reading.

Your personal and professional habits will probably stay with you for your entire career. If you have your act together and are perceived as having your act together, you will make a positive impression, which will help predispose the clients and the partners favorably before they start to evaluate your technical skills. Good work habits will give you a clear and open playing field, which will permit you to utilize your technical skills without obstruction. Looking at it negatively if you must, remember that a lost piece of paper can cost you your job.

You need to develop a reputation for efficiency. Think about it. Would you like to work with someone who does not take particularly good care of his or her clothing, works in a paper-strewn office, is known to let a typo slip through now and again, is often late or pressed to meet two deadlines at once because of poor planning, and grumbles about having too much to do and not enough help? Or would you prefer a colleague who looks good, keeps files moving efficiently across the desk, proofreads all work (being a stickler for accuracy), shows up on time, exudes efficiency, and meets requests for help with a good word and a smile? It is not much of a choice, is it? And that kind of impression can last for years.

6

WATCH YOUR FLANKS

A new lawyer in a 20-lawyer South Bend firm spent the last few dollars in his pocket to bring flowers to his secretary when he reported to work. A few weeks later, a partner—in the exercise of pure ego—dumped a huge research project on the new associate with an unreasonable Monday deadline. When the appreciative secretary found out, without being asked she arranged to have two other secretaries help over the weekend. One found a file and research memorandum prepared by another lawyer two years earlier, which was a wonderful start. The other two typed and copied until ten o'clock Sunday night, and the project was on the partner's desk Monday morning.

But that is not all. Four years later, that demanding partner advanced the associate's partnership candidacy.

A law firm is by nature a strange beast. You have a collection of highly educated, aggressive owners of a business, all of whom are interested and involved in seeing it prosper. Because of that interest, there are as many viewpoints on what is necessary to succeed as there are partners. Each partner feels with some justification that as an owner, he or she has the right, even the obligation, to make decisions regarding the future of the organization. After all, he or she owns the business. All this means that the firm is an almost impossible organization to manage ("law firm management" is an oxymoron!), and the managing partner should be remembered in your prayers, preferably on a daily basis.

This also means that you will receive conflicting messages about your future, the firm's future, the partners, and clients. You name it, you can get a conflicting message on it. The best remedy will be to "receive and file," then move on with your business.

YOUR CO-WORKERS

Get to know as many people in the firm as possible—partners, associates, legal assistants, secretaries, clerks, messengers. Of course, if you are in a big office or multioffice firm, that will be harder to do. But introduce yourself. No one is too important to be intimidating or too unimportant to be ignored. Get to know first names and use them.

Partners

Seek out the partners unobtrusively. Introduce yourself. Try to get to do work for as many partners as you can, so they know you and your work. As you meet partners in the real estate or corporate practice groups, suggest you would like to work in those areas "sometime" if that is where your interests lie. Offer to help when you know they are under particular pressure, if you have time to help.

Use this approach intelligently. If you are in a big firm, do not practice out of your practice group or call partners in other offices. Remember to be unobtrusive.

Likewise, do not rush out the first week and try to line up 17 assignments from 17 partners. Take it easy and in stride. Follow the rules. Work through the chain of command or your supervising lawyer.

As you attend social functions of the firm, introduce yourself to partners and the spouses of partners you have not met. Sit with people you see only occasionally or hardly at all. If you do not have the opportunity to work together, establish a personal relationship. In other words, use the firm's social functions for your own political purposes. In reality, that is what they are intended for—to enable everyone in the firm to get acquainted.

Meet spouses as well as partners because although lawyers are not to discuss client or firm matters at home, partnership candidates are often the exception to the rule. Now, do not run off to practice being Uriah Heep (or Eddie Haskell for the unread!). Spouses do not make decisions. I am just suggesting that having a familiar name and face cannot hurt.

Support Staff

You should pay as much attention to the support staff. Get to know all the clerks, messengers, secretaries, and supervisors. And I mean know them—who they are, about their family, about the evening course they are taking or the wedding planned for next year. Use their first names, and encourage them to use yours except when persons from outside the firm are present. Do not worry that being so informal will make your status in the pecking order less secure. Support staff are painfully aware who the lawyers are and that the law-yers rule. You do not need to remind them. Be gracious.

Do so primarily because knowing everyone is a nice thing to do and will make the office a nice place to be. But also, the support staff can make you or break you. There will come the day when you need a special favor to look good in a client's or a partner's eyes. It is much easier to ask a favor of someone you know than of someone you have been ignoring in the hallway. It is possible for the ignored to ignore.

Distinction: The Need for Discretion

An important distinction must be made here. Be friendly and open, but be discreet. Discretion will take all sorts of forms.

You must adhere to the strictest ethical restrictions regarding client confidences. There is never an excuse for mentioning anything about a client's affairs to any-one outside the office. This includes everything from whispered tales in the bedroom to veiled references on a crowded elevator. Nor should you broadcast client matters within the office beyond a need-to-know basis. You may know a spicy tidbit, but by telling everyone, you test persons who may not know or understand the significance of the disclosure or the importance of the ethical restrictions. Further, your broadcasting of such information very likely will be viewed unfavorably. Quite simply, it looks unseemly.

It is also ill-advised to talk about people in the office. Know about people. Be interested in their interests, families, and concerns. But do not become the central clearinghouse for all office rumors. Do not even contribute to the rumor data bank. On the contrary, discourage the practice. If you are aware someone is under unusual personal pressure or not feeling well, it is a charitable act to alert the appropriate supervisor working with the individual, but no more. If you know someone is acting contrary to ethical, legal, or firm strictures, you have an affirmative obligation to report the activity to the managing partner, practice group, or office leader, but no one else. You can never be viewed in a good light as a rumor monger. It will never help; it can only hurt your partnership prospects.

If you hear rumors outside the office about the firm, one of the partners, a client matter, or some business decision of the firm, you should report the rumor. It is acceptable, if you are affected, to ask for clarification. But go to someone involved in firm management who should know and who is likely to be able to provide any data you need.

This can be very ticklish. Address such issues gingerly. If you have no legitimate reason to interject yourself into a situation, do not. Just listen. One way or another, sooner or later, the truth will come out. Until it does, just stay clear of the topic and avoid the minefield.

Under no circumstances should you comment negatively on other associates in the Partnership Sweepstakes, their abilities or lack thereof, their work product, their practice development prowess, their political views, their personal problems. Only have kind words—you can find something nice to say about everybody. Be helpful and endeavor to make everyone look good. If someone is not carrying his or her weight, it is not up to you to advertise or correct the problem.

Your responsibility is to make the client and the firm look good. Someone else will take care of the slacker. You never know who is who or exactly what role someone fills. There is no mileage in commenting on your perceived competition, only danger.

I know I am taking all the fun out of office politics by saying that you should not talk about all the juicy matters floating around. However, you certainly have an obligation of candor to the firm. As I stated before, some matters must be reported to management. Likewise, you have an obligation to respond when asked for information by legitimate authority in the firm. Be a lawyer and choose your words. Differentiate between fact and hearsay.

A LITTLE HUMILITY, PLEASE

When you have successes in your practice, balance crowing and humility. It is better to have someone else spread the gospel of your victory at trial, big deal closed successfully, or new client landed. But if no one else does it for you, it is perfectly acceptable to report facts. Do so with all the humility you can muster.

As a variation on the last guideline, follow the practice of sharing credit, not blame. That is, when things go right, speak up with regard to others' contributions. Let everyone know which other lawyers and legal assistants helped on the matter. Personally and publicly give your secretary and other members of your support staff credit for their contribution. That often goes further than anything you can do for any team member. To many, it is worth more than a raise.

But if things go wrong, do not point your finger at others to indicate someone else lost the case or made the mistake. While you do not need to beat your breast and wear ashes over a loss or a mistake, do not blame anyone else either. Probably no one will believe you. It certainly will look unprofessional. If a mistake is legitimately someone else's, handle it quietly through channels. Advise your supervisor in writing. Putting your comments in writing is critical because it will force you to choose your words very carefully.

If you do not know how to handle the situation because blame can be shared all around or because of political considerations, seek guidance from a friendly partner, a "Dutch aunt or uncle" who is not involved with the client matter and can advise you dispassionately.

Any critique you deliver should be delivered quietly and in private, not to others or in a public place. No one wants to hear via the grapevine that you were dissatisfied with his or her work product. Be direct, quick, clear, and unemotional. Then move on with the job.

For more guidance on supervising support staff, see Kenneth Blanchard and Spencer Johnson's book, *The One Minute Manager* (New York: William Morrow & Co.) In reality, you are managing the team on projects and should know good management techniques for the process.

PROSPER THE TEAM

Another important aspect of personnel relations is the team. You should be dedicated to the prosperity of the entire team—the staff, the other associates, and the partners. In other words, you should do your utmost to engender harmony, to get everyone to work as a team, to make everyone look good. This is the third time I discuss team building. Does that tell you how important it is?

Teamwork is an ongoing and long-term effort that takes many forms, from the obvious and unusual to the quiet and mundane. Here are some suggestions:

■ *Smile.* Any assignment can be made easier with a smile, a positive attitude, a can-do approach. Try it; it is infectious. If you, like me, were born smileless, it will take effort. You have to convey your smile in other ways—by your disposition, your greeting, your tone of voice, the cookies you bring to the team members. It all matters, though it is not always easy, particularly when the going gets tough. But that is when it is needed all the more.

■ *Say please and thank you.* It is amazing what common courtesy can do to instill enthusiasm in your colleagues. It too is infectious. It shows respect, and every member of the team, from senior partner to office messenger, deserves respect as an individual and for his or her contribution to the team effort. Your acts of courtesy should be warm and sincere; do not simply go through the paces to satisfy form. A mere show of politeness will not work, at least not for long.

■ *Do not lose your temper.* Do not curse or use vulgar expressions. Very little can be improved upon by an eruption of emotions. You will certainly make an impression, but most likely you will regret it. Foul language is distasteful to many people, but it is unlikely you will ever know. You will simply find that your co-workers give you a wider berth and you are a little less a team member.

■ *Volunteer.* As I have said before, be willing to step in cheerfully to help someone get the job done. Remember that sooner and better for everyone is sooner and better for you, too. I am not suggesting that you go around doing others' job assignments for them, but in order for the firm to produce on time, you may be needed to do a job normally reserved for someone else. For example, from time to time, I go for the coffee or run the photo-copier. It is good for the soul. (This presumes, of course, that the task at hand is the most important part of the team effort that needs to be done at the moment and that I am available to do it.)

■ *Do not ask someone else to do a job you are not willing to do yourself.* Although work in the office should be assigned to support staff designated to handle particular matters, you should be willing to type, photocopy, deliver, file, or whatever is paramount at the moment. The occasion when you will actually do so will be rare if your office is properly staffed and organized, but you should have a mind-set that makes you willing if necessary. Your law degree does not put you above doing any job. Each job deserves respect, and each worker is entitled to self-esteem.

If a job is particularly distasteful—and that can happen in the handling of physical evidence or marshaling the assets of a deceased client—be willing. If you are supervising staff members, appreciate their efforts, express that appreciation, and help if necessary. Do not hide. Do not be aloof.

▪ *Learn how to use the office equipment.* Some midnight or weekend you may be the hero who can unjam the facsimile machine, log on to the local area network, or transfer that urgent call from the switchboard.

These ideas are simple, but they are how a team is built and how you get into the starting lineup.

PERSONAL MATTERS

The handling of personal matters for yourself is a ticklish issue. Some firms are very opposed to staff members helping with a lawyer's personal matters, no matter what the problem may be. Other firms permit staff to deliver dry cleaning, schedule social commitments, pick up children at day care, balance checkbooks, or do Christmas shopping—all on the theory that the lawyer will then have more time for billable work. Some staff members are happy to help; others may view it as demeaning and insulting.

You should first find out what your firm's policy is. As with any policy question, find out from management, not your fellow associates who may not know or who may be skating close to the line themselves. If the firm permits such assistance, proceed cautiously, and do not risk setting new standards for brass. If you overstep the line in the mind of some senior statesperson who has a say in your future, that is a tough reputation to live down.

If help with personal matters is not a problem for your firm, then be sure to check carefully with the staff person you are asking to provide a favor. At any sign of reluctance, back off immediately. You may offend.

SUGGESTIONS FOR IMPROVEMENTS

There is no human endeavor that cannot be improved upon, particularly in a law office. Chapter 3 already discussed suggesting new practice areas, but as you develop as a practitioner, you will probably notice other things about the office, its policies or procedures, that can be improved.

Convey your suggestions to the appropriate authority, but do so carefully. You do not want to be perceived as saying that someone's pet project is a pig. First, find out whose domain you are entering. If you do not already know, determine whether the authority being approached is normally receptive to suggestions. If so, ask for a free moment. Be pleasant. Say you have a suggestion. Make it cautiously. Ask whether it has ever been tried before. Share credit immediately if appropriate. If the authority is receptive, ask to develop your idea, perhaps in writing. Volunteer to pursue the idea and its implementation.

If you do not receive a favorable response but are convinced that the objections raised should not knock your idea out of consideration, press once. If you still do not succeed, back off. Thank the listener for listening—even if he or she is not and did not—and withdraw. Do not be a pain . . . even if you are right.

If you do not succeed the first time, or the second or the third, try when the idea light goes on again. You will always get credit for trying, for thinking, and for having the firm's practice at heart. But do not go overboard; instead, think and proceed with moderation. You do not need to lead the "Idea of the Week Club." Remember, the ideas have to be good ones, and you have to be politic. The firm presumably is reasonably well managed—at least, the people to whom you are speaking think so.

Further, remember that your goal should be, and be perceived as being, to make the firm better. You should not be perceived as simply trying to garner attention. That will happen with any honest effort. You do not need to worry about getting appropriate credit.

If I were to boil this chapter down to one thought, it would be that you should focus on what is best for the firm, its practice, clients, lawyers, and staff. If that is your focus, this chapter serves as a list of suggestions on how to express it, how to show others that it is first in your career thoughts. In the end, if you achieve that, your career will be well served.

7

BEHAVE YOURSELF

Three lawyers—friends from their law school days in New York City—met for lunch. Two of them were partners at the same San Francisco firm. They told the third lawyer about one of the associates in their firm who was having an affair with his secretary. Although broad-minded about most matters, the partners concluded that the associate had just written off six years of effort with the firm. Cheating on his wife and subjecting the firm to possible claims of sexual harassment showed such an obvious lack of judgment that the associate's chances for partnership were gone.

This chapter will really grate against the more independent-minded, freethinking associates. But you need to know how you and your behavior inside and outside the office will be perceived. You may not like what I say, but the comments in this chapter will pertain to almost all law firms, large and small. So please read on, even if I appear to be conservative or narrow-minded.

If you want to make partner, the simple fact is that your behavior inside and outside the office should be beyond reproach. The partners will not distinguish between what you do (or do not do) in the office or in public. In their eyes, either reflects on the firm, whether you think so or not.

In today's legal marketplace, lawyers are very competitive and protective about their client relationships. They do not want clients to worry about anything other than receiving the best legal services at a competitive price. That alone is tough to deliver. Any distraction caused by the inappropriate activities of a firm's lawyers does not help the cause and will not be well received.

I am speaking of your personal behavior, not about pro bono activities that may offend the political sensitivities of some clients. I hope that your firm has matured to the point of supporting its lawyers' legitimate activities, properly pursued. If not, you have a real problem in the firm for which you decided to work. (In that case, take time to cool off and look at the matter as objectively as possible before making any rash moves. Ultimately you may have to either make a decision based on principle or eat that principle to keep your job—not a happy choice. All I can say is, seek older, wiser, and disinterested counsel.)

CHEMICALS

I know a lawyer who successfully landed a new client by refusing to imbibe. The client repeatedly suggested a drink before their introductory lunch but later stated that he would not have retained the lawyer if the drink had been accepted. You may never be tested in this unorthodox fashion, but do not drink alcoholic beverages at luncheon if you are working after lunch. Likewise, do not indulge at any time if you are expected to provide legal services at the same time or later the same day. Do not worry about explaining. Simply say you do not drink if you are working. No one will object.

Do not drink to excess at any time. And do not drink and drive. You may be in complete control of your faculties, but you also may not pass a Breathalyzer test. If you flunk, no explaining you can ever muster will be sufficient. Simply put, you were DWI, and that will never be forgotten at the firm. It will always be a cloud, a doubt in the minds of some of the people in a position to elect you a partner.

Do not use drugs, and do not experiment with drugs. The same rationale regarding alcohol applies. In addition, if you find yourself in a situation where others are using drugs, get out. If you were there when the user OD'd or the authorities arrived, you would never be able to explain yourself adequately in the minds of some of the partners.

SEX IN THE OFFICE

Avoid any office sexual liaisons. Sleeping with or cohabiting with another person from the office, be that person a lawyer, legal assistant, or staff member, will not remain secret for long . . . if ever. I guarantee someone will not be happy with the news.

Avoid any notorious sexual liaisons outside the office. It may be your life, but the partners, rightfully or not, think they own it and do not want it to reflect poorly on the firm. The partners do not want people asking, "Is that the kind of people that firm hires?" or "Does the firm condone that kind of behavior?" The partners' concern may or may not be a matter of morals. It is more likely an issue of public relations. And you will lose.

All cautions aside, office romances do occur. If you find yourself in one, and it is real, then check the office policy on nepotism and make an appointment to see the managing partner. It is much better to be forthright and to discuss how your romance will be addressed by the firm. If it presents a problem, management will work with both of you to resolve it. I know of firms that prohibit nepotism and in such situations have worked to relocate one of the individuals or have waived the rule.

The most difficult part of an office romance is guarding your behavior in the office. You must avoid spending time together behind closed doors or at the water cooler (if it still exists). You must remain businesslike, perhaps going to extremes to do so. If your romance is with a superior or a subordinate, you must be especially cautious. Perhaps you should pursue a change of assignment to avoid the appearances inherent in such a situation before management makes the suggestion. It is toughest, even impossible, in a small office.

Remember that problems may arise in spite of your perfectly appropriate behavior, because you cannot control the reactions of the jealous or the small-minded. Be cooperative.

SEX WITH A CLIENT

Even more dangerous than an office liaison is an affair with a client. Some states regulate sexual liaisons between lawyers and their clients as ethical matters.

Your fiduciary duties to your clients include the duty to avoid undue influence, as well as the duty to keep a clear mind for dealing with the client's problems. An emotional entanglement can cloud your judgment.

If a client makes a pass at you, it is best to decline to become involved while the lawyer-client relationship exists (do so politely and save as much face for the client as possible). If this happens, report it to the firm's management immediately. In this way, you can protect yourself in case the client does not accept your rebuff graciously.

PERSONAL PROBLEMS

If you have family problems, try to keep them out of the office. That can be difficult, because you cannot control every situation or the people with whom you share the problem, but try. Do not share your problems with staff members or even other lawyers, except on a need-to-know basis. Otherwise you will be fueling the rumor mill to your own disadvantage. Be assured that no one can keep a secret.

If a personal or family problem is likely to affect your work—and almost all problems do so at some time—tell management. You do not need to provide all the juicy details, just the fact that the problem exists. Thereafter advise when the problem comes to a head, is resolved, and so on, so that management knows how long allowances must be made.

Do not worry; we all will have such problems from time to time. Do not try to hide them, just address them in a businesslike fashion. (We will return to the issue of personal problems in Chapter 8, on client priority.)

DARE TO BE BORING

Avoid any form of outrageous behavior. You can no longer get away with what you may have done in college or law school . . . presuming you got away with it, that is! I guarantee, someone will not think it is funny.

If I were to summarize this chapter in one sentence, it would be, "Dare to be boring." If you are to stand out from the crowd, make it because of your technical skills, client handling, or civic involvement, not because you are a personnel problem or an embarrassment.

If the message of this chapter arrives too late because you have already created a problem, then clean up your act. Fly straight and impress everyone with how you have matured. Doing this may take significant effort and some time, but it can be done. You must be acceptable enough so that your proponents among the partners have enough to hang onto when advancing your cause for partnership.

If you have had a problem or created one, you may wish to find out whether it will damage your prospects for partnership. First, let some time pass so the dust settles and any emotions cool. After several months or even a year, ask someone in authority whom you believe to be a mentor about your partnership prospects. Ask in a businesslike way, and be ready to accept the response without emotion.

The problem with the answer is that if you are told your prospects are dim, you know they are and should consider leaving. If you are told all is well, the information may be inaccurate (unintentionally), but you do not know it. I do not have any magic answer to this dilemma. All you can do is look to the normal indicia of advancement: status moves, compensation, etc.

Do not run around the firm asking every partner about your prospects. You can ask only once unless advised to ask again. Otherwise, you will create a problem for yourself, perhaps where one did not exist.

8

PUT THE CLIENT FIRST

A sole practitioner from Houston lost a court case after months of preparation and a trial that went on for weeks. He had been representing one of his best corporate clients, who had paid him faithfully each month during the pendency of the matter.

The lawyer did not relish the thought of visiting the owner of the company. But when he did, he was stunned. The client offered her condolences and expressions of support. By knowing what was transpiring every step of the way, the client said, she knew how hard the lawyer had worked on the case and how intent on winning the lawyer had become.

Winning would have been much better, but the client felt well served.

Your ethical obligations to clients are of paramount importance. In addition, there are many other ways in which the client must come first. Some of these are crucial; others are mundane.

ETHICS

If you took a good ethics course in law school—which I hope you did—you already know that the legitimate interests of the client come before the interests of the firm or even your career. That standard will be very difficult to apply as you run in the Partnership Sweepstakes. Everybody tends to get wrapped up in the pursuit as it progresses. Do not let it happen.

Remember, priority goes to the *legitimate* interests of the client. Unfortunately, a client sometimes asks a lawyer to do something that is ethically, morally, or legally prohibited. Do not be trapped by your desire to please the client. Consult with your supervising lawyer, the partner in charge of the relationship, the chair of the firm's ethics committee, or the managing partner— whoever will address this new problem. By asking you to do something improper, the client has placed your obligation to the law, the profession, the firm, and yourself above your obligation to the client.

You must work at knowing the ethics of the profession. Read the Model Rules of Professional Conduct. Know the Model Code of Professional Responsibility. Follow the ethics rulings just as you do the advance sheets—regularly and in depth. Instinct is helpful, but you must know the technical rules as well.

If you are with a good firm, a serious slip from the correct ethical standards will be fatal to your candidacy. As with misbehavior in your personal life, no explanation is sufficient. If an ethical departure is of no moment at your firm, you should reconsider whether you really want to be a partner there. If you do, you and your firm deserve each other, and the profession is poorer for it.

QUALITY

A crucial—and very basic—way to put the client first is to deliver high-quality services. This means that you and all who work with you must put forth your best effort.

Do Only Your Best

You must be satisfied that you have researched completely, drafted well, and attended to all the details. You must use all the firm's quality assurance systems to make sure conflicts are avoided, specialty work is done by appropriate specialists, opinions are double-checked, the proper forms are used, documents are accurate, and deadlines are met. To use these systems, you must know and understand them. Only if you do so can your motivation to put the client first be of any benefit.

The client deserves the best you can provide even if that takes too many billable hours and therefore is uneconomic for the firm. Any decision regarding the economics of doing the best job is addressed as part of accepting an engagement or in the billing process, not as part of the rendition of services. Once you have taken on a matter, you must do your best, no matter what the cost. As Chapter 4 mentioned with regard to timekeeping practices, leave the economic concerns to those more senior to you.

By all means, discuss your concerns with the billing partner. Provide your analysis. Learn from the experience. But still do your best.

Tolerate Only the Best from Others

Those working with you, be they support staff or other lawyers, must know that you will not accept anything but the best. Chapter 5 mentioned this before when discussing work product. It is not acceptable to put out the brief without an available argument because "I did not get to it." A document containing errors may not be mailed. The details must be double-checked. Be a stickler.

Develop a reverence for quality work, and project it to all. Not everyone will like you all of the time for this attitude, but everyone will respect you. That is better.

PERCEPTIONS OF QUALITY

The tone of this chapter has been pretty lofty so far. But client satisfaction is an everyday battle in the trenches as well. Let me make some simple suggestions you can incorporate into your daily practice habits.

Although a top-quality work product done in a timely and efficient manner is a sine qua non, the client seldom is knowledgeable enough to know that. However, the client does know whether he or she is receiving prompt attention, courteous service, and empathy. In addition to the hints suggested in Chapter 5, here are some thoughts on how to convey a sense of quality service.

Telephone Calls

Return all phone calls promptly, certainly on the same day received. If you know you are going to be unavailable, have your secretary, receptionist, or message center tell callers immediately when you will be available to return calls. If your staff promises you will return a call at a particular day or time, be sure it gets done on time or even earlier if possible. If you find out too late that you are not going to be able to return a call the same day, have the client called back, apologized to, and told when you will be available.

The client should be asked whether the matter can await your return. If not, another lawyer should be asked to handle the call, or you should be interrupted wherever you are. No matter what closing, trial, or seminar you are at, there are really few days that you cannot take a break at some point to return an urgent call.

I have returned many a phone call from airports, hotel rooms, and conference rooms of other law firms. I often ask or have my secretary ask a client if I may return calls from my hotel room or my home, late at night if necessary.

It is tempting to ignore or put off calls from unpleasant clients. But if you do, they will just get more unpleasant. Nothing makes a client more upset than being unable to reach you. If you have trouble dealing with difficult people, a number of books provide techniques. Also, the partner whose client this is has probably developed an arsenal.

The client should get the idea that his or her call is very important and that in spite of your unavailability, you and your staff are bending over backward to accommodate his or her needs.

Know how your clients are being treated by your secretary, receptionist, and others who handle the phone. Make sure the interchange is pleasant and informative. It should be formal but not stiff. All the social niceties should be honored. Efforts to accommodate should be obvious. A touch of humor, if not forced, may help.

The support staff should identify with the client's need to find you and "work it out together." Staff should offer to find you so you can return the call, rather than provide a number where you can be reached. It saves the client from the aggravation of being bounced around as a hotel or, worse, another law firm tries to find you. This also gives you some control because you determine when you can best return the call during your trip, closing, or seminar.

If you are to adequately represent your client, sometimes making or returning a telephone call just once is not enough. When you know the client's matter is urgent, you may have to pursue the other party, the other party's lawyer, or even your own client to make progress. "He or she did not return my call" is a pretty weak excuse if you called just once. Dogged pursuit, if appropriate, is impressive to the client and to your own firm's partners. Appropriate is the key word. Your calls must be geared to the importance and urgency of the subject matter. Again, you must balance—balance between getting your job done efficiently and just being a nuisance to or being perceived as a nuisance by the client or the partners. If you have doubts, seek counsel from a seasoned lawyer.

Opposing Counsel

Whether you are involved in litigation or negotiation, a closing or a telephone call, treat opposing counsel courteously. Many new lawyers are trained or decide on their own that zealous representation of a client means constant hostility toward opposing counsel. Bar association surveys list this as a leading source of lawyer dissatisfaction with the profession.

But these are often the same people who can refer business to you or from whom you may need a time extension or other permissible favor some day. And judges do not appreciate lawyers who refuse to agree to reasonable requests from opposing counsel. If you are not courteous and easy to work with, word will get around to other lawyers, and you may be sure that your behavior will be returned in kind. This will not serve your client well.

Correspondence

Send clients copies of all correspondence and documents prepared for them as their matter progresses. Make sure your secretary understands that this is your standard operating procedure, so that it happens automatically. Your clients may not know or understand everything you send, but it gives them a basis for asking questions. As in the opening vignette, advising your clients of your actions will also remind them that you are attending to their problems. When they get a bill, they will not be surprised by work descriptions with which they are unfamiliar.

Time Sheet Entries

If you have billing responsibility, review all time entries regularly so that nothing said is embarrassing or will come back to haunt you. When you are preparing time entries, read each one as the client would read it.

Avoid shorthand. Instead of "conference client," add the topic(s) discussed. Instead of "prepare documents," specify which documents or parts you prepared.

Avoid entirely "review file" or "look for file." Those are invitations for clarification that lead to an impression that you are inefficient or sloppy or both. Remember, the impression is supposed to be that you are attentive, thorough, efficient, and dedicated. Make sure your time entries and those of others on the bills you review bespeak just that. Your client deserves this much and will have less to be concerned about. The client will be able to focus on the legal problems, rather than the person solving them.

Office Politics

I am back on my favorite topic again. Keep office politics to yourself. The client is not interested or should not be. If confronted with a question, duck. Disclaim knowing details, then change the subject.

If the client wishes to pass along a compliment regarding your work, provide him or her with the proper name to call or write. Do not solicit client endorsements, however; that fact will get back to the firm and will not help your cause. You will be faulted for bringing a client into a firm matter.

Personal Problems

As I have said before, keep personal problems to yourself. The client is paying for your counsel, not vice versa. If a personal problem is going to interfere with your ability to provide services, first advise your supervising lawyer at the firm to determine how the work should be handled and explained to the client. If explanations to the client are called for, keep the details to a minimum.

Investments

Be very careful about investing in a client's business. First, know the position of your firm on the subject. An economic tie can cloud judgment or lead to a conflict of interest. If it is permitted, make sure your particular proposal receives all necessary approvals. Understand that at the first hint of a problem, you have to be willing to take whatever steps are necessary to make the problem go away. Generally, such investments are best avoided.

Keep in Touch

Touch base with clients regularly as you develop ongoing responsibility for their matters. If you have not had a new matter in a while, just call to check in or have lunch. This becomes increasingly important as you start to introduce new clients to the firm or existing client relationships are entrusted to you. You must make sure clients have no doubts that you want and enjoy their business. You will have to ensure that others in the firm are following the hints outlined here to create the same good impression.

That is the basic message of this chapter. Your client and others in your office must know that you put the client's legitimate interests above all others. The client will rest easier. The other lawyers and support staff will know that is your standard and will act accordingly. They will try to do as you do. It is infectious. Good examples always are. That helps you, because the partners will recognize this in you and will want you to be part of their practice.

9

GET INVOLVED

A young lawyer in Buffalo practices in a four-lawyer firm. Much to the surprise of some older lawyers, she recently developed a national profile over a two-year period because she took on a bar committee assignment no one else wanted. She researched the area, wrote an article, then organized a CLE seminar. The topic suddenly became hot when there was Congressional testimony to give. She turned out a book and now is a recognized authority.

No doubt she will soon be a partner in her firm or have her pick of partnerships to join.

Law practice has always produced people who are involved in public affairs. Perhaps it is a personality flaw that compels so many of us to be involved with government, civic panels, and various other community leadership positions. It is not a recent phenomenon in this country; it goes back at least to those pushy lawyers who signed the Declaration of Independence.

Personality flaw or not, being involved in your community, your church, your school, or whatever is an important contributing factor for you in the Partnership Sweepstakes and throughout your career.

Now, let me clarify that I think every lawyer has a duty to the community. After all, you have the skills that can be helpful, and you will be benefiting in a big way from that community. You owe. You owe big. But you bought this book for the crass reason that you thought it would help you make partner, so I am putting this issue in those terms.

While I am convinced of the benefit of community and professional involvement, it is necessary to maintain a balance throughout your career. It is important to be involved in professional activities as well as community activities. Let me address the professional activities first.

BAR ACTIVITIES

The various bar associations afford you an opportunity to learn as well as contribute to the improvement of the profession. I do not know of any bar association that would not welcome a new contributor to the cause. The potential benefits are significant.

If you are in law school, join the Law Student Division of the American Bar Association. If you are fresh out of law school, consider the Young Lawyers Division of the American Bar Association and/or the comparable committees or sections of your state bar association. Once you have started to specialize, consider the various sections and committees that are devoted to your specialty. Most bar groups will have them.

Initially you may have to be a "gofer" for the more senior members, doing their bidding in committees and on projects. But ultimately you will be able to participate in writing articles for publication, studying the impact of proposed changes in the law, lecturing, and lobbying for legislation. All this will help you develop as a specialist, because you will be on the leading edge of the law in your chosen field. You will become a better lawyer. You will become an authority within your firm.

It is not difficult to become involved with the various bar associations. As I said, I do not know of anyone who has ever been turned away. You can start within the firm if there is a partner who is active and can put you in touch with friends or acquaintances in the bar. Likewise, other lawyers in your community whom you know to be active usually will be quite helpful. (Lawyers do not tend to be as competitive with each other when it comes to bar activities.) If nothing has worked so far, take the direct approach and call the area delegate for your state bar or the American Bar Association. That person certainly will have the names of the lawyers who can get you involved on the committees you want.

It will cost you (or your firm) to join the bar groups and the appropriate sections. The investment is worthwhile. If your firm does not automatically provide such membership as a benefit, ask for yourself. There is no harm in asking, and the benefit will certainly accrue to the firm.

Consider joining your local and state bar groups, as well as the American Bar Association. While you will probably not have time to be very active in all three, there are still benefits. The American Bar Association and your state bar have educational materials produced by the various sections which will be helpful to you until you decide to become active.

Your local bar association may have some excellent educational activities, but that will not be its prime benefit. Local bar groups are the best way to get to know your colleagues in a nonadversarial atmosphere. When the time comes to cross swords, it is nice to have rubbed elbows first.

Aside from the formal association, most locales have bar groups dedicated to the proposition of having fun. They sponsor tennis tournaments, golf outings, picnics, dinner dances, and theatrical endeavors, often for the benefit of charity. Again, this is a great way to know and to be known. Participating will help you in your practice.

One day you will need an extension of time to file the reply brief or permission to forward a document after rather than at a closing. Those courtesies will come much more easily when you have socialized with the lawyer on the other side.

COMMUNITY ACTIVITIES

Community activities are just as important, but for very different reasons. When I say "community activities," it is an umbrella term intended to include church, school, alumni, and every form of civic and charitable endeavor, from coaching a team of disadvantaged youth to playing in the community orchestra, from raising funds to fight disease to serving on the board of directors of your zoo. All these activities produce benefits. They all count.

Where to Start

Most community groups are open to permitting new volunteers to join their cause. You must be willing to join, to serve on a committee, to attend meetings, to do paperwork, to make telephone calls, to ask people for money. You will probably have to start in the trenches as a volunteer doing some or all of these activities before you will be asked to join the board of directors of any organization.

Your church and various school alumni groups are always hungry for workers. They are a good place to start. Just ask the appropriate leadership how you can help.

For other organizations, use the resources of your firm to provide introductions or arrange appointments to groups. If lawyers in your firm are active in your community, there will be a network in place which you can access. Use it. Clients can also help if you learn of their involvement and have a similar interest. (There is a danger in asking a client to make such a contact for you, which I will discuss later under "You Must Perform.") If the firm or clients cannot help, a call to the organization itself will usually work.

Benefits of Being Active

There are numerous benefits to being active in the community. As I stated before, the benefit to the community is foremost. Secondly, there is a feeling of personal satisfaction in knowing you are providing this benefit. But from the selfish viewpoint of this book, there are also numerous positives.

Your personal profile in the community will be enhanced. You will be known by more people and will know more people. That permits you to show off your abilities as a lawyer. It also spreads the news of you as a lawyer. The people you meet will have the opportunity to ask you to help them with their legal problems.

You will be able to work alongside business and political leaders in the community, learning about their businesses and local developments, sometimes before they occur. You will start to form a personal network quite apart from that of the firm.

Your personal profile in the firm will be enhanced. Word will get around that you are active in the community. People within the firm will ask to access your network as they learn about it. (Always permit free access through you. A network only works if you use it, doing and receiving favors. People like to be asked to help and like being able to receive assistance.)

You will enhance the image of your firm. Outsiders will comment about your community involvement to the partners, and the partners will take pride in that. Try to use the firm name as much as possible as you undertake your community activities. It is easy to do.

- Use the firm's stationery for the letters you write as you fulfill your board responsibilities. (Be sure to check your bar association's advisory opinions limiting the use of a lawyer's letterhead for the solicitation of charitable contributions.)

- Add the names of the other volunteers to your mailing list for the firm's announcements and newsletters.

- Whenever your name is used in any press release or organization listing, be sure your firm's name appears also.

You will attract new business to your firm. People generally pick as lawyers people they know or have had the opportunity to see in action. In this case, the action may be as informal as a business conversation at a cocktail party or a discussion of a community activity's business problems at a committee meeting.

It is important that you know many people and constantly make new associations. In this way you have a constant flow of new opportunities to be retained. Although a cocktail party or a country club tee may provide these opportunities, community activities do it better. Whether raising funds, writing letters, or discussing problems, you are doing lawyer-like things more regularly. You display your personal efficiency, your organizational skills, your writing and speaking abilities, your personal moral code, and your ability to relate to people and their problems. None of that can be achieved on the tee, much less with a drink in your hand. (I am not an old poop; there are practice development opportunities in your sporting and social activities. I just do not think they are even close to being as extensive or effective as community activities.)

YOU MUST PERFORM

I hope it does not need saying, but it is imperative that when you undertake any bar or community activity, you handle it as well as any client matter. You will achieve all the benefits only if you perform well. Colleagues in professional groups and volunteers in community activities do not distinguish your performance on client matters from what they see you do in other activities. They will assume you are as good (or bad) in your professional life as you are in the bar or community involvement they observe.

There is much justification in that view. After all, if you are efficient, you are efficient. If you are a good writer, you are so all the time. Why should people assume otherwise?

So you must attend the meetings, be on time, stay until the conclusion, have assignments completed on schedule; work must be well organized; telephone calls must be returned promptly. In other words, all the recommendations applicable to client matters apply here too. If you are not going to be able to meet these standards, it would be better not to take on the particular responsibility in the first place. As in client matters, you develop a reputation for good performance over a long period of diligence . . . and lose it with just a few screwups.

You must also be willing to take leadership positions with respect to the bar or community activities. If the activity helps you and your practice, a leadership position helps more. The profile is higher. There are more opportunities to meet potential clients or referral sources. You will move with other leaders more often. Your network will be more extensive, and you will have more clout.

SPREAD THE NEWS

Once you are involved, there is another way to benefit your practice. Bring the activity into the office. There is nothing wrong with letting others know of your activities.

If your firm has a newsletter, announce any committee appointments, chairmanships, or offices attained. Offices of all sizes have a bulletin board.

Let the partners know of your activities. They will appreciate the network you are developing and may wish to access it. If they do, all the better for the firm and for you. From time to time, casually discuss what you are doing on bar committees or fund-raising campaigns with partners over lunch or walking up the street to court. But as I have said before, your "crowing" should be discreet and selfless: Discuss the importance of the work, not your importance.

Seek volunteers in the office to join you in your endeavors. All lawyers should be involved in the bar association, so give them a chance. Everyone—lawyers, legal assistants, staff members—should be investing time and effort in the community. So ask for help with fund-raising campaigns and activities or for volunteers to act as docents at your museum. Do not be pushy; just make the opportunities available via a memo, the newsletter, or more casual conversations. I know of a small firm that adopts a charity each year to which the lawyers and staff contribute their efforts—all as the result of the interest of an associate (now partner).

Having company from the firm as you work on an auction for your public television station or a walkathon for the March of Dimes will improve your relationships in the office. The firm will get more notice as more personnel are involved, and you will be noticed as the leader of your firm's effort.

NETWORKING

Much of this chapter comes down to the concept of networking, to which I have referred several times. By networking, I mean having a group of friends and acquaintances in all walks of life in your community or around the country, people with whom you have some regular contact and to whom you can turn for a favor, information, or another contact, and who can turn to you for similar consideration. We all have networks. The idea I am advocating is that you should have a large, multifaceted network and should work to keep it fresh and growing.

A network can atrophy quickly unless it is maintained. Bar activities and community activities are one good way of doing this. Other ways are mailing lists (which I will discuss later), the occasional lunch or telephone call, even the greeting card at holiday time.

Another thing about a network is that it works best when it is used. People enjoy being asked to do a favor, provide information, or make a contact, so do not hesitate to do so. At the same time, encourage others to rely on you. Stated crassly, you build up chips, which can be used in the future. A healthy network means you owe and are owed, and the stacks of chips are regularly going up and down.

Your network will include clients, but not just clients. You will have nonclients who make referrals, as well as people who will never make a referral but who will be able to put you in contact with a government official or check a reference for a client. A network serves all sorts of purposes.

The purposes served may be yours personally, clients,' those of other network members, or, hopefully, those of the partners and clients they are servicing. Helping a partner through your network is a dynamic way of demonstrating your value to the firm. Always be willing; always be discreetly doubtful whether your network can resolve the problem, so as to avoid creating expectations; always pursue your network vigorously but appropriately; and always add the partner who is helped to your network.

Networks never meet. They do not generate reports or minutes. They do not take on projects as an organized entity. The only formality is your personal telephone directory. You never ask someone to join your network or volunteer to join somebody else's. You just participate by knowing people and by being known.

POLITICS AND GOVERNMENT SERVICE

Politics and government service can be an important component of your networking effort. Consider making political campaigns part of your community endeavors. Whether the candidate you assist wins or loses, that person will not forget and someday may be of assistance to you or your client.

Political involvement may not change the outcome of your request, but it will probably assure access to the government office, bureaucrat, or legislative committee needed by your client. Politicians usually lose a race or two before they win. And many who do not win end up in bureaucratic positions of influence. Thus, the effort is usually ultimately worth the investment.

When getting involved politically, be sensitive to the political persuasions of your firm. Some firms are very Republican or very Democratic; others try to maintain a balance. If you support a Democrat and all the partners are Republican, you are taking a chance of alienating some of the partners. If the firm gets substantial business from Republican party sources, consider whether you are at the correct firm for you or whether you want to be politically involved on the other side of the aisle. Be sensitive; test the waters.

WHAT DOES THE FIRM THINK?

The concept of testing the waters applies to your bar and community activities as well. As I have said, it is quite easy to get involved. It is also possible to get overinvolved. For your own protection and in keeping with your basic goal of achieving a partnership, you should do two things.

First, plan your activities wisely, allowing for all the activities of your personal and professional life. Remember that you must do an equally good job at each of them. Knowing what time you have for bar and community activities, fill the gap with the activities most important to you. Plan ahead, since committee or board terms are often multiyear. Make sure the meetings and other obligations fit into your calendar. Make sure you can do the jobs undertaken without cheating the firm, its clients, your family, or yourself.

Second, if your activities will infringe on the time you should be devoting to practice, seek clearance from the firm. Firms and partners view such endeavors with varying levels of acceptance or encouragement. You should know where your firm stands and the views of your supervising lawyer. You want to enhance your partnership chances, not run counter to everyone's wishes.

If your firm is like most, the partners will want new associates to start slowly, so the partners can observe how well you handle the responsibility and how well you represent the firm. Also, they will want you to place primary emphasis on developing your technical skills as a lawyer. As you progress and succeed as a lawyer and with your bar or community activities, you will be afforded more time to undertake more of the same. If new clients are a side benefit, you will be aggressively encouraged to do more.

Another reason you should seek clearance for your activities is to solicit financial support. If you must travel for bar association committee meetings, will the firm reimburse you? If you chair a fund-raising drive, will the firm make a contribution? May you host a meeting in the conference room with the firm providing luncheon?

Most firms have stated policies or established practices with respect to such matters. But if yours does not, do not be afraid to ask or offer to split the cost. The answer you receive will tell you to a certain degree how enthusiastic the firm is about such outside activities.

If the firm does reimburse expenses and support charitable endeavors, do not abuse the policy. Spend the money more carefully than you would your own. Obtain specific prior approval for substantial expenditures. Always obtain receipts, and promptly and completely account for sums spent.

If the firm does not support your endeavors, you will have to proceed more judiciously and as your own resources will allow. I still think it is worth it; you just have a rather shortsighted firm.

10

MARKET

A middle-aged couple had engaged the Santa Fe firm to handle the purchase of a large residential property. In the course of waiting, first at the bank and then at the county building, the associate had plenty of time to ask questions and to discover that the couple had no children and no estate plan. Having seen a partner use the tactic before, she suggested that an estate plan was appropriate, given the magnitude of the investment they had just made, and that the firm could make some fee accommodation, given the cost of handling the closing.

The clients readily agreed, and the firm's estate lawyers found themselves planning a multifaceted estate exceeding $10 million.

In Chapter 8, I tried to convince you that clients and their interests are the most important items on your career agenda. But there is more that you should do with clients in order to develop a good professional relationship and prosper your interests as well as theirs.

There is nothing wrong with that thought; you are entitled to succeed, too. As long as the legitimate interests of the client come first, you can and should prosper right alongside the client. This requires marketing skills in addition to lawyering skills. Therefore, this chapter is devoted to the topic of marketing your abilities and the expertise of the firm to old, new, and potential clients.

I will provide some suggestions on how you do just that. Several have been made before, such as knowing a client's business or orienting a team to the client's interests. That is because good practice habits *are* good marketing. And much of what good marketing requires serves the client well also. So I will repeat some concepts but from a marketing perspective this time.

As you read the specific principles, keep in mind that successful marketing is closely tied to the proper treatment of clients and their matters. You can and should have more than one motivation for treating clients properly: They are paying for and deserve the best treatment, and the best treatment is the best way of generating more work. No one will care whether you call it quality services or good marketing, as long as the client is well served. You are helping the firm and enhancing your chances for making partner.

MIND-SET

Your mind-set should include treating existing clients as if they are new clients just won over to the firm who must be impressed as you handle the firm's first assignment. Clients are most often lost because a lawyer becomes presumptuous about the relationship, not because he or she has mishandled the matter technically. If you always treat your clients as new clients, they will notice and will enjoy working with you.

THE TEAM

Explain to legal assistants and support staff the nature and importance of the services you are rendering to each client. It is part of the team building discussed in Chapter 6. Keep them, as well as the partner in charge of the particular client account, fully abreast of developments and the specific work you are doing.

Treat the partner in charge as your client. The partner should always know what is happening. That way the partner is never embarrassed in front of the client. The partner looks good. The firm looks good. You receive points for efficiency.

KNOWLEDGE ABOUT THE CLIENT

Keep yourself informed about the client, its particular problems, industry, and current trends. Know the client's products, services, and markets. Visit the client's offices, plant, or facilities on your own time. In other words, show the interest that convinces clients of their importance to you. Pass on this information to others in your organization, so they can help fuel this impression. This approach will raise your stock as a real client's lawyer.

It is important to know both the good news and the bad about clients. I mentioned it in Chapter 3 with the thought that it is necessary for good representation. Full knowledge is also an excellent way of developing good client relations. For representation purposes, you need to know about contracts landed, expansions, layoffs, quarterly financial results, and any matter that will affect the services needed, influence the client's perspective, or provide an opportunity to cross-sell.

The more you know about the client, the more work you will be able to identify, the more problems you will find, the more suggestions you will be able to make for improvements the firm can provide. This effort will be largely unbillable time. But it will help you generate more billable hours for you and others in the firm.

CROSS-SELLING

Cross-sell services provided by you and by others in the firm positively and discreetly. The opening vignette shows one way this can work. Provide introductions to other lawyers, describe skills and expertise enthusiastically. Offer a benefit. The impression should be that you want to make things better for the client. Only with the prior approval of the billing partner, offer to take a quick look at a problem without financial obligation on the part of the client.

FRIENDLY RELATIONS

Become a friend to your clients, and treat them as friends. Socialize, go to a luncheon or dinner, attend sporting or cultural events, play golf, etc. It is a good practice to send clients cards or handwritten notes congratulating them on promotions, weddings, birthdays, and births. Keep a record so you can catch the birthday next time around.

But as I said in Chapter 8, do not share your personal problems with clients. That level of intimacy requires a lot of friendship. If you guess wrong, the client can lose confidence in the intensity of your focus on his or her problem.

Be sensitive to the appropriateness of client friendships. As a young associate, you are not likely to become the close friend of the CEO of a major publicly traded company or an executive twenty years your senior. Rather, pick your peers in the client ranks. You will be able to communicate better, have more in common, and have the potential for a long-term friendship to nurture. When people on the way up ultimately get there, they usually help those who struggled along with them on the way.

ENTERTAINING CLIENTS

The appropriateness of entertainment also speaks to what you do with clients. Entertainment should not be "on the cheap"; that shows a lack of regard for the person entertained. Likewise, it should not be exorbitant, which only proves you are making too much money on the client's matters. Do what you know the client likes to do, and do it in a manner that is comfortable and consistent with your life-style.

Include the client's spouse whenever possible. It is a great way to win a friend in court.

Never entertain at any event or in any fashion that could be deemed to be in questionable taste. You guessed it—no strip joints, either male or female, even if the client asks. You both may have fun, but someone up one of your respective ladders may not like it at all . . . and you may never know.

MEETING AND GREETING

Every public function or social activity is an opportunity to meet potential clients. Treat it as such. First, behave as suggested in Chapter 7.

If asked, tell people you meet that you are a lawyer and mention the firm name. A great way of getting that information on the table is to ask the other person about his or her job/career first. Do not come across as a pushy lawyer on the make. Do not start discussions of your career and your firm; rather, try to get your new acquaintances to start providing that data about themselves. Ask questions, and be interested in what you are told.

If your conversation leads to questions on legal problems or issues, avoid giving legal advice. Rather, offer to check into the matter and offer your card to the person asking. Tell the person you look forward to hearing from him or her, and turn the conversation back to discussing something of interest to your new friend and potential client. Stick close to the person so that your refusal to give an opinion is not interpreted as a brush-off.

If you do not get a call within a few days, call your prospective client and offer to discuss the problem. You will know quickly enough whether the person was serious about needing legal services for which he or she was willing to pay.

POSITIVE ATTITUDE

Whether at a social function or while being grilled by your mother, always be positive and upbeat about the firm, the lawyers at the firm, the firm's culture, and your work. That sends a strong signal about your receptivity to taking on new work. Indicate you are busy but not overloaded. If you are overloaded at the moment, say it will soon pass . . . and then go back to read Chapter 4 about managing your work levels.

When given an opportunity to discuss the firm, work in comments that indicate the nature of the practice and the sophistication of the services being rendered. Of course, do not talk about specific projects or clients. Even referring to matters on a no-name basis creates problems, because you never know all the interests of all your listeners or whether they know enough from other sources to figure out which client you are referring to. Such a result would be disastrous. Instead, speak in generalities so that nonlawyers can be impressed with the firm, its practice, and you.

Be careful not to oversell. You should not be selling every time you open your mouth. You do not want people to head the other way when you come by because they expect you are going to be peddling your firm's wares. There is nothing so boring as a boorish lawyer.

Be positive about your community and its institutions. Look for and expound upon the good to be found there. The vast majority of people like their hometown and have favorite institutions. You will win friends along the way.

Be positive. The world is full of critics. We as lawyers all too often are paid to be critical, to look for the risks, for the liabilities, and for what is wrong. You should belie that role, that reputation, and be recognized as someone who is upbeat, positive, and constructive. That will instill clients and potential clients with confidence that you can resolve any problem, solve any dilemma. They will want to bring you their problems.

MAILING LIST

Develop a mailing list for firm announcements, newsletters, white papers, holiday greetings, and the like. That list should include all your contacts, members of your sorority or fraternity, your law school class, family members, members of bar committees and community boards on which you serve, and clients including each individual with whom you work—the entire network described in Chapter 9 and then some. Everyone with whom you have had contact is a candidate for your mailing list. A mailing list is a good, simple way of reminding clients that you consider them important, and of letting potential clients know that you are a knowledgeable lawyer who would appreciate their business.

Mailing lists require monitoring. Fresh out of law school, you will have a limited number of listings. But as you practice and become involved, you must add new names. That should be a regular, periodic exercise. Your secretary should be keyed into the process so he or she can do much of the adding for you. Likewise, if you lose contact with people on your list, consider dropping them after a period of time, perhaps two years.

KNOWLEDGE ABOUT YOUR COMMUNITY

Monitor developments in your community, looking for an opportunity to send a congratulatory note upon someone's promotion, election to any position of responsibility, or honor. Send those notes only to people you know personally. Include the clipping that appeared in the press with a brief handwritten thought.

As you send notes, cards, and gifts, it is a good idea to inform any partners who have a relationship with the client or potential client. Just send a photocopy of your note to the appropriate partners with an interoffice cover memo indicating that you thought they should know. This prevents a partner from being embarrassed if your kindness is mentioned. It also demonstrates to the partner your client-minding and marketing skills. That is good for you in the minds of the client and the firm.

KNOWLEDGE ABOUT MARKETING

Read. Much is being written on the subject of law firm marketing. There are books, tapes, newsletters in profusion. Most likely your firm will subscribe to one or more. I have given you just a smattering on the topic, and you should keep current by reading and perhaps attending a course from time to time. You might start with the books on marketing published by the American Bar Association's Section of Law Practice Management.

There are always new ideas and developments in marketing. Just as you do in your practice specialty, you have to work at keeping current.

THE FIRM'S MARKETING PROGRAM

Take an active role in the firm's organized marketing effort. Depending on the size and nature of the firm and its plans, you may start out by doing research for newsletter articles or white papers, glad-handing at firm receptions, or sitting at the firm's table at civic luncheons and dinners. Do these things enthusiastically and frequently.

As you become more senior, you may also become involved in planning practice development or making presentations to prospective clients. Again, leap at the chance; seek it out with the appropriate partners. You want to convince the partners that you have a marketing bent. You want an opportunity to pass on the ideas and information you have gleaned from your readings on practice development.

Committee participation will also permit you to flex your network (discussed in Chapter 9) by helping younger associates to become involved in civic or bar activities with which you have developed ties. Practice development committees often work at developing the firm's network.

You may feel more comfortable doing certain aspects of marketing than others. If you are a "people person," you will probably thrive on the receptions, civic luncheons and dinners, and all forms of client entertainment. If you are more retiring personally, you may prefer the research and writing for the firm newsletter or a white paper, or handling behind-the-scenes arrangements for practice development functions. No matter what you prefer, force yourself to do some of each type of work. "I am not good at that" is usually true for lack of practice.

No matter how you become involved, participate in the firm's institutionalized marketing efforts in some way. If you are not asked, go ask what you can do. And ask over and over again.

Whether we like it or not, marketing and client development are where it is at these days in our profession in firms of all sizes. There was a time when the rendering of quality services was enough. Clients have discovered that most communities have several good lawyers who can do the same thing equally well. Image, profile, reputation, personal relationships, and all those marketing-based issues are becoming determining factors. You may be a better lawyer technically than Associate X. But if Associate X has a client following, a billing list, a book of business, and you do not, the X brand will win every time. "But that is not fair!" Sorry.

RELAX, RELAX, RELAX!

He had been expecting partnership this year. The requisite number of years had gone by. He knew his work had been good, and a few new clients in the past year had added the cream. The partners' wives had systematically been his dinner partners at firm outings. He had even been forced to push and claw, aggressively at times. He knew that he had stepped on his competition, but to him it didn't matter: he wanted to make partner.

But when he was called into the managing partner's office after the partners' annual meeting, he knew by that partner's obvious discomfort that something was wrong. He had missed by one vote. Last year's class of two new partners had voted against him.

Go back and reread Chapter 2. Then come back here, and I will say it again.

Have you ever been at the park and observed the enthusiastic little rascal who charges out on the soccer field and immediately starts kicking everything in sight: the kids on the other side, teammates, the officials, and, only occasionally, the ball? When he does make contact with the ball, it does not always head in the appropriate direction.

From the day you walk in the door of the firm to the day you are elected partner, you must appear as relaxed and confident as possible regarding your career and your partnership candidacy. On the other hand, while you must put on that face, you should be ever attentive to the myriad concerns I have outlined in this little book. Further, although my analogies refer to games of chance, the quest for partnership is not a game and should be taken seriously, not flippantly. It is all a balancing act that you must execute with grace.

Enthusiasm is always welcome and wonderful. The secret in your campaign for partnership is to focus your enthusiasm on your daily activities—your practice and all the matters I have outlined. That will show you off as a heads-up, technically skilled, aggressive lawyer, well prepared, looking to make rain, active in the bar and community, with concern for clients, and with practice habits to support that concern.

PREPARE A PERSONAL SCHEDULE

To properly focus your enthusiasm, you have to plan and schedule the suggestions I have made. Make up checklists of what you think you should be doing now and what will come later. A sample appears in Appendix B. Do not try to do everything at once. I have covered everything an associate should do over the five to ten years that, depending on your firm, it generally takes to attain partnership.

I am assuming admission to a general partnership, which is still the real measure of accomplishment and acceptance in a firm. There are junior partnerships, nonequity partnerships, and contract partnerships. Call it what you will, you are an employee until you become an equity partner. In my view, you are capable of and should be functioning as a partner after five years. By that point in your career, you should be clearly on track and the partnership question should be when, not if.

Keep your checklist to yourself, but use it, review it regularly, and update it periodically. Make sure you are addressing all items at the appropriate time.

The appropriate time is tough to assess without knowing you and your firm. As you are doing your planning, consult with the partner with whom you are working: "Can I get involved with a bar committee?" "May I make arrangements to take Client X to a baseball game?" "I would like to do volunteer work with the Multiple Sclerosis Society if you think it is OK." "Do you think we should take Client Y to lunch to find out if she is satisfied with our services?" It is rare that any partner will discourage you. Most will let you take on matters as you feel comfortable doing so.

If you run into some ol' #*!-#!* who is negative on everything you suggest, consider asking someone else. If your practice area administrator says no, do not hesitate to mention your next idea to another partner with whom you work or to the managing partner. No complaints, just a new venue. Eventually you will get what you want or something reasonably close. If you continue to receive negative responses, consider that you may be pushing too far or too fast, or perhaps both, and back off.

It will come. It may take time. No matter. This is a long campaign, not a pitched battle. Let it develop naturally. If you have adopted the correct personal approach, the partners will notice and will give you what you need. It will become a two-way street.

DO NOT COMPETE

Other associates will help you along the way, and you should try to reciprocate. You are not and should not be in competition with them for partnership. You will achieve much more by winning friends and inspiring trust from the other associates. View the race for partnership as comparable to your tests in school. Everyone can get a passing grade, and if you help the other associates, you will have friends for life who will be wonderful to have as partners. Even if someone is elected a partner, passing you by in the sweepstakes, smile genuinely, wish him or her well, and be sure friends know you are happy because of the new partner's success. That is how collegiality builds in a firm.

Never, never step on someone else or rejoice in another person's setbacks. You may be wrong. It looks unseemly. It damages the atmosphere in the firm. The other person may reciprocate.

A PRESUMPTION

This whole book presumes that your firm exercises good faith and operates morally and ethically in affording partnership opportunities to its associates. I cannot write otherwise, and there is no way you can predict and perform otherwise. If that is not the case with your firm, this book is of little value as a road map to partnership, and you should consider finding a new firm where what you have read will be helpful. You will never be happy where you are, even if you do attain partnership. It is like winning with crooked dice or a stacked deck.

How do you know whether the firm plays by the rules? Well, how does it treat its clients? Does it abide by the Model Rules of Professional Conduct? Do not expect any better treatment. A firm is not going to be forthright and fair with you while it cheats with everyone else.

You will not need much time to find out. The signs are usually apparent. If there is a problem on a client's matter, is the client told? If too much is charged on a client's account, is the bill adjusted? If a conflicts issue arises, is it addressed and resolved, or is it ignored? The signs are there.

I am sorry to have to write this section, but some members of our profession are not as honorable as they should be. Avoid them. They are generally known among the practicing bar, and there is nothing they can do to enhance your reputation or your career.

IT MAY NOT HAPPEN

Even if you do everything I have prescribed in this little book plus some other good twists of your own, you still may not make partner. There are no guarantees. There are too many imponderables, too many factors over which you have no control but that will affect your partnership candidacy: the financial fortunes of the firm or its major clients, deaths and early retirements, new lateral partners, and old clients lost.

If you cannot affect such factors, do not worry about them. Just keep working on what you can influence.

Your effort and devotion to these suggestions will not be lost. Along the way, by doing everything prescribed here, you will have become an excellent lawyer. As such, you will be readily marketable to every law firm, large and small, in town. You will be welcomed with open arms and possibly as a lateral partner.

CONCLUSION

Wherever you go, I hope you do well. The law is an honorable profession. If you do as I suggest, you will be an honorable and contributing member.

I do not really believe that to make partner in a law firm, you have to be quite as calculating as I have depicted. I was just appealing to your prurient interest to get you to keep reading. That way I could get across the points that will make you a better lawyer.

Good luck!

QUESTIONS YOU COULD HAVE ASKED WHEN INTERVIEWING WITH A FIRM

During interviews with law students, law firms usually focus on training, departmental rotation, salary and fringe benefits, client contact, specialization, work allocation, and other aspects of associate life. I will not try to outline all the questions you could ask. Rather, this appendix focuses on the issues interviewees usually forget or do not know to ask.

There are no correct answers to these questions, but the answers will tell you much about the firm and its culture. You will know whether you are going to work for a dictatorship, a Greek city-state, or something in between. Then you can determine whether this appeals to you.

Only two general questions cover the whole cultural issue. For each I have listed subquestions, which indicate the type of information that the general question is intended to obtain.

In asking this type of question, you must be discreet. If the firm's representative seems comfortable and forthcoming with answers, press on diplomatically. But if you sense discomfort, be prepared to change the topic.

1. *How Is the Partnership Structured?*

   - How are partners selected?

   - Are all partners general partners?

   - Are there contract, junior, or nonequity partners?

   - If so, how do they fit into the structure of the firm?

   - Are they involved in decision making? Do they have complete access to all firm information?

   - Is there mandatory retirement for partners? If so, how does it work?

2. *How Is the Firm Governed and Managed?*

   - Is there a managing partner?

   - If so, is he or she the CEO?

   - How is the managing partner selected?

   - Is there a governing body?

   - If so, how is it selected?

   - Are there qualifications for partners to serve?

   - Do members of the governing body have a limit on their terms of service?

   - Does the governing body determine partner compensation?

B

TO-DO LIST FOR THE PARTNERSHIP SWEEPSTAKES

This list maps out a strategy for winning the Partnership Sweepstakes after five years as an associate. There is no magic to this list. It is not hard and fast. It is not even a recommendation. Rather, it shows a possible approach for one individual.

Everyone will have a unique list. Yours may be in a different order. Some items may come sooner, some later, and some not at all. Associates in your firm may make partner in three years, or it may take six.

No matter. The purpose of the list is to give you an idea of the progression that occurs. Then you can develop your own list, factoring in the elements particular to your firm and your individual abilities.

As you develop you list and see that some areas are proceeding nicely while a few are trailing behind, you will know where to place your emphasis and your energy. Your list therefore must be fluid, allowing you to respond to opportunities presented or changed circumstances. You must seize those opportunities, no matter how early they arise. And you must adapt to those circumstances, even if doing so puts you behind your schedule.

Just keep growing. That is the magic.

Year 1 — Get Started

- Orient yourself to the firm via the associate manual, policy memos, etc. Ask for a mentor.

- Set a time budget for the year. Monitor your performance.

- Organize your calendar and telephone directory.

- Decorate your office.

- Check your personal wardrobe.

- Read *The Wall Street Journal* and the business section of the local newspaper regularly.

- Read one or two publications covering news of the profession.

- Increase your technical expertise by reading advance sheets, taking CLE courses, and using video and audio cassette programs.

- Start a mailing list with family, personal friends, law school classmates, sorority and fraternity members, etc.

- Volunteer to attend civic luncheons and dinners, fund-raisers, bar functions, etc., on behalf of the firm.

- Join the Young Lawyers Division of the ABA, the state bar association, and any local bar association.

- Volunteer to do research for the firm newsletter or a white paper.

- Take a vacation.

Year 2—Push On

- Volunteer to participate in the firm's recruiting program.

- Volunteer to assist with firm receptions or other organized practice development activity.

- Serve on a committee of the ABA Young Lawyers Division.

- Start to work with particular clients, get to know client operations, read about industry developments to keep current.

- Serve on a civic, church, or alumni committee. Do some fund-raising or coaching, or run activities.

- Do everything you did in Year 1, and enhance it all.

Year 3—Keep Going

- Add to your volunteer activities and start to seek board memberships.

- Join a bar association committee in the area of your specialization.

- Entertain clients, particularly counterparts in corporate organizations. Start with luncheons.

- Do everything you did in Years 1 and 2.

Year 4 — You Are Almost There

- Add a second or third board membership.

- Write a law review article in your specialty.

- Add a second bar association committee or take on more responsibility on your existing committee.

- Schedule more client entertainment, assuring adequate coverage, and staying within budget.

- Write for the firm newsletter.

- Volunteer to be a mentor for a new associate.

- Do everything from Years 1, 2, and 3.

Year 5 — It Is "When," No Longer "If"

- By now you are acting at the partner level.

- Entertain clients at dinners, sporting and cultural events, according to client preferences.

- Consider joining a private club for client entertainment purposes if appropriate for your firm, your practice, and your community.

- Develop a client following and your own billing list.

- Seek offices in civic and bar committees.

116

- Make a presentation in your specialty as part of the firm's in-house training program.

- Do everything from Years 1, 2, 3, and 4.

INDEX

Selected Books from

THE SECTION OF LAW PRACTICE MANAGEMENT

Access 1991-1992. Has been thoroughly revised to reflect the many new changes in the legal automation world since the 1989-1990 edition. Many new publications, user groups, vendors, seminars and conferences are listed. All entries have been reviewed and—where necessary—updated.

Action Steps to Marketing Success. This book will show you how to turn your marketing ideas into action. You'll learn how to run an ongoing, coordinated, results-oriented marketing program. Numerous forms and sample letters included.

Basics for Buying Your Personal Computer. Will help you ask the right questions and evaluate the right issues. Facts and advice on components, servicing, networking, features to consider.

Basics for Writing Your Law Firm Brochure. Gives advice for planning and creating a brochure. Includes samples of brochures produced by other law firms.

Beyond the Billable Hour. A collection of articles on the subject of alternative billing methods, including value billing. Contributors include small, medium, and large firm practitioners, consultants, and general counsel.

Designing Your Law Office: A Guide to Law Office Layout and Design. Guides you through the entire process. You'll learn how to avoid needless disruption, chaos, and cost overruns. Includes checklists, timetables, diagrams, and drawings.

Fast Forms with Macros: Document Assembly with Word-Perfect 5.0/5.1 (and 4.2). This product, which includes a booklet and diskettes, gives step-by-step instructions that will help you develop your own customized, automated substantive systems — using WordPerfect 5.0 and macros as the basic building blocks.

Flying Solo. A collection of 48 articles discussing major aspects of starting, managing, and maintaining a successful solo practice.

From Yellow Pads to Computers. 35 chapters with real-life computer applications that focus on practical solutions. Especially for the attorney who's been too busy or afraid to use a computer.

How to Start and Build a Law Practice, 3rd Ed. Jay Foonberg's classic guide has been updated and expanded. Included are more than 10 new chapters on marketing, financing, automation, practicing from home, ethics and professional responsibility.

Identifying Profits (or Losses) in the Law Firm. The latest book in the Financial Management Monograph Series. Designed to help firms identify profits (or lack thereof) by their source.

Improving Accounts Receivable Collection: A Practical System. This book will give you the basics for developing an *easy-to-manage, formal* billing and collection system that can cut *months* off the collection process.

Keeping Happier Clients. This book is your guide to better client relations. It describes a whole approach to building strong relationships with clients. Includes questionnaires and tips for follow-up.

LOCATE. Includes listings of law office computer software vendors with indexes listing applications and package names.

Managing Partner 101: A Primer on Firm Leadership. Advice from the corner office that will help any new or aspiring manager. Described as an "indispensable, no-nonsense handbook."

Marketing Your Practice. A complete guide for planning, developing, and implementing a law firm marketing plan. Includes checklists, questionnaires, samples of brochures and newsletters, direct mail pieces.

Practical Systems: Tips for Organizing Your Law Office. It will help you get control of your in-box by outlining systems for managing daily work.

The Quality Pursuit: Assuring Standards in the Practice of Law. This multi-author work provides perspectives on a wide range of issues related to quality assurance and high performance standards, including dealing with the problem partner, partner peer review, training programs.

Winning with Computers. This book addresses virtually every aspect of the use of computers in litigation. You'll get an overview of products available and tips on how to put them to good use. For the beginning and advanced computer user.

Withdrawal, Retirement and Disputes: What You and Your Firm Need to Know. Suggests how you can deal with, or even avoid, the snafus that accompany partner departures. Also discusses how your firm can institutionalize fair and workable policies related to withdrawal, disability, and retirement.

Writing Your Law Firm Newsletter. Get rules and guidance for writing a newsletter, including tips on graphics, timetables, cost-benefit analysis. With sample newsletters created by other firms.

Your New Lawyer. A complete legal employer's guide to recruitment, development, and management of new lawyers.

Order Form

Quantity	Title	LPM Price	Regular Price	Total
_____	Access 1991–1992 (5110297)	$29.95	$34.95	_____
_____	Action Steps to Marketing Success (5110300)	29.95	34.95	_____
_____	Basics for Buying Your Personal Computer (511-0221)	14.95	24.95	_____
_____	Basics for Writing Your Law Firm Brochure (511-0223)	14.95	19.95	_____
_____	Beyond the Billable Hour (511-0260)	69.95	79.95	_____
_____	Designing Your Law Office (511-0263)	59.95	69.95	_____
_____	Fast Forms with Macros (511-0269)	99.00	109.00	_____
_____	Flying Solo (511-0084)..	39.93	44.95	_____
_____	From Yellow Pads to Computers, 2nd ed. (511-0289)...............	64.95	69.95	_____
_____	How to Start & Build a Law Practice, 3rd. ed. (5110293)	32.95	39.95	_____
_____	Identifying Profits (511-0259)...........................	14.95	19.95	_____
_____	Improving Accounts Receivable Collection (511-0273)...	39.95	49.95	_____
_____	Keeping Happier Clients (5110299)	19.95	29.95	_____
_____	LOCATE 1991–92 (5110295)	59.95	69.95	_____
_____	Managing Partner 101 (511-0272)	19.95	29.95	_____
_____	Marketing Your Practice (511-0215)	44.95	54.95	_____
_____	Practical Systems (5110296)	24.95	34.95	_____
_____	The Quality Pursuit (511-0268)	74.95	84.95	_____
_____	Winning with Computers (5110294)	89.95	99.95	_____
_____	Withdrawal, Retirement (511-0211)	29.95	39.95	_____
_____	Writing Your Law Firm Newsletter (511-0216)....................	14.95	19.95	_____
_____	Your New Lawyer (511-0075)	39.95	49.95	_____

Handling Charge $3.95

Total $ _____

☐ Check enclosed   ☐ Visa   ☐ Mastercard   ☐ Bill me

Account Number _____ Exp. Date _____

Signature _____

Name _____

Firm _____

Address _____

City _____ State _____ ZIP _____

IMPORTANT: A phone call will speed your order if we must contact you: (_____) _____

Return to: American Bar Association, Order Fulfillment 511, 750 N. Lake Shore Drive, Chicago, IL 60611

If you need overnight delivery, call 312/988-5555

BOOK

CUSTOMER COMMENT FORM

 THE SECTION OF
LAW PRACTICE
MANAGEMENT

Title of Book: _____

We've tried to make this publication as useful, accurate, and readable as possible. Please take 5 minutes to tell us if we succeeded. Your comments and suggestions will help us improve our publications. Thank you!

1. How did you acquire this publication:

☐ by mail order   ☐ at a meeting/convention   ☐ as a gift

☐ by phone order   ☐ at a bookstore   ☐ don't know

☐ other: (describe) _____

Please rate this publication as follows:

	Excellent	Good	Fair	Poor	Not Applicable
Readability: Was the book easy to read and understand?	☐	☐	☐	☐	☐
Examples/Cases: Were they helpful, practical? Were there enough?	☐	☐	☐	☐	☐
Content: Did the book meet your expectations? Did it cover the subject adequately?	☐	☐	☐	☐	☐
Organization and clarity: Was the sequence of text logical? Was it easy to find what you wanted to know?	☐	☐	☐	☐	☐
Illustrations/forms/checklists: Were they clear and useful? Were there enough?	☐	☐	☐	☐	☐
Physical attractiveness: What did you think of the appearance of the publication (typesetting, printing, etc.)?	☐	☐	☐	☐	☐

Would you recommend this book to another attorney/administrator? ☐ Yes ☐ No

How could this publication be improved? What else would you like to see in it?

_____
_____
_____

Do you have other comments or suggestions? _____
_____
_____

Name _____
Firm/Company _____
Address _____
City/State/Zip _____
Phone _____
Firm Size: _____ Area of specialization: _____

We appreciate your time and help.

Fold

NO POSTAGE
NECESSARY
IF MAILED
IN THE
UNITED STATES

BUSINESS REPLY MAIL

FIRST CLASS   PERMIT NO. 16471   CHICAGO, ILLINOIS

POSTAGE WILL BE PAID BY ADDRESSEE

AMERICAN BAR ASSOCIATION
PPM, 8th FLOOR
750 N. LAKE SHORE DRIVE
CHICAGO, ILLINOIS 60611–9851

Fold